SONGS FROM THE

SONGS FROM THE

WITH

PAUL WINSLOW

**SIMON &
SCHUSTER**

London · New York · Sydney · Toronto · New Delhi

A CBS COMPANY

First published in Great Britain by Simon & Schuster UK Ltd, 2012
A CBS COMPANY

1 3 5 7 9 10 8 6 4 2

Simon & Schuster UK Ltd
1st Floor
222 Gray's Inn Road
London
WC1X 8HB

www.simonandschuster.co.uk

Simon & Schuster Australia, Sydney
Simon & Schuster India, New Delhi

A CIP catalogue for this book is available
from the British Library.

ISBN 978-1-84983-673-9

Typeset by M Rules
Printed and bound by CPI Group (UK) Ltd, Croydon, CR0 4YY

Contents

Introduction

If you want to know why Chris Martin is not in Coldplay, why it's better to be a sausage than an egg, why your mother is wearing Tupperware or why Ambrosia custard is not important then you're in the right place. Welcome to *Songs From The Barmy Army*.

During 18 years of touring the globe, England's famous band of travelling fans has entertained (and occasionally annoyed) the world of cricket with a wide variety of compositions. Some are sophisticated, witty songs explaining in graphic detail cricketing happenstance. Others are complete and utter nonsense that would have Freud coming out in a cold sweat if he ever tried to work out the hidden meanings behind them.

From the bars of Barbados to the pubs of Perth and the stands of Sri Lanka, we are delighted to bring you, for the first time ever, the complete songbook of the world's greatest sports fans. But it's not just the songs themselves, we bring you the stories behind them and the reactions they have elicited from the players who have been serenaded and the fans who have done the serenading.

We also get under the skin of the songwriting fraternity, asking some of the most prolific lyricists how they go about writing a Barmy Army song, what makes a good one and how they get it off the ground. And no musical round-up of the Army's activities would be complete without mention of Billy the Trumpet, so we've snuffled around his extensive catalogue to bring you the ten best Bill tunes.

The Barmy Army phenomenon started with a few fans singing a small selection of chants during the 1994–95 Ashes tour. They were mainly aimed at the Australians as a way of responding to the abuse they were getting as England lurched from one defeat to another. As it snowballed, the chanting evolved into songwriting, and in the early days many of the tunes were imported from the football terraces.

But the songs then took on a life of their own, and more sophisticated tunes were composed specifically with the cricket team in mind. Soon there was also a move towards writing songs for individual players as opposed to the team in general. The nature of that evolution is traced in this book, so come with us as we take you on a journey through the back catalogue of cricket's premier songwriting fraternity.

1 ASHES SONGS

They are the songs that started it off. And they're the songs that carried it on. The classic anti-Australia songs have stood the test of time, and on every Ashes tour a new generation of fans, both Australian and English, revel in the humour for the first time, while old-timers who have sung them countless times on multiple Ashes tours never tire of them. The Barmy Army travels the globe, but nothing gets the juices flowing like an Ashes series and a bit of Aussie-bashing.

'BALL AND CHAIN'

'We came here with backpacks, you with ball and chain' is the original Barmy Army chant that actually came to prominence during the 1992 World Cup in Australia. A chap by the name of Monty Cotton brought it to the Test match party and little did he know what he was starting. The line quickly became infamous and was used on the inaugural Barmy Army T-shirt. Three years later, Andy Evans sat entertaining people with his rendition of The Animals' classic 'House of the Rising Sun' and got to the line about 'ball and chain'. A eureka moment followed and so the song and the chant were brought together in perfect harmony.

(to the tune of 'House of the Rising Sun')
There is a house in New Orleans,
They call the Rising Sun
It's been the ruin of many a poor boy
And God, I know, I'm one

One foot on the platform, one foot on the train
I'm going back to New Orleans, to wear my ball and
      chain
One, two,
BALL AND CHAIN! BALL AND CHAIN!
We came here with backpacks, you with ball and chain

BALL AND CHAIN! BALL AND CHAIN!

We came here with backpacks, you with ball and chain

WHAT THEY SAY

'So we sparked that up, us and some lads in Nottingham Forest shirts, and we walked past the Aussie fans on the Brisbane Hill, dragging our feet as though we were in balls and chains. When we got back to the tea bar, the pocket of England fans watching us – there were probably only about 40 at this point – gave us a standing ovation.'

— Dave 'The General' Peacock remembers the moment a phenomenon began.

'CONVICT COLONY'

The Grim Reaper is a nickname that will never be forgotten in Barmy Army circles and his legacy is further cemented by this composition that will be sung for as long as England tour Australia.

(to the tune of 'Yellow Submarine')

In the town where I was born
There lived a man who was a thief

And he told me of his life
Stealing bread and shagging sheep
So they put him in the nick
And then a magistrate he went to see
He said: 'Put him on a ship, to the convict colony'

You all live in a convict colony
A convict colony, a convict colony
You all live in a convict colony
A convict colony, a convict colony

WHAT THEY SAY

'You can see what effect the Barmy Army has had on the Australians – they hated it. The opposition see you as a threat.'

— Matthew Hoggard

'THE AUSSIES LOVE THE ENGLISH'

The Barmy Army will happily belt out 'God Save the Queen' on occasion, but it's been usurped by 'Jerusalem' as our favoured 'national anthem'. However, when it comes to reminding the

Aussies of the fact that they still have the Queen as head of state (and voted to keep her in that role in a referendum in 1999), we're more than willing to break it out, with a big intro and a subtle change.

(to the tune of 'My Old Man's a Dustman' and 'God Save the Queen')

The Aussies love the English
You might find it quite strange
'Cos we sent them all Down Under
With only balls and chains
And when they see the English
They always shout and scream
But when they had the chance to vote
They voted for the Queen

God save YOUR gracious Queen
Long live YOUR noble Queen
God save YOUR Queen (you're a convict)
Send her victorious
Happy and glorious
Long to reign over YOU
God save YOUR Queen

WHAT THEY SAY

BARMY ARMY

'Ladies and gentlemen will you please be upstanding for the Australian national anthem.'

— Dave 'The General' Peacock often likes to leave out the intro and get straight down to brass tacks with 'God Save Your Queen'.

'I SHAGGED MATILDA'

If there's one song that's guaranteed to amuse and annoy the Aussies in equal measure then this simple, clever and slightly risqué rendition of their unofficial national anthem is guaranteed to do the job.

(to the tune of 'Waltzing Matilda')

I shagged Matilda, I shagged Matilda

I shagged Matilda and so did my mates

And she moaned and she groaned

And she took it up the billabong

I shagged Matilda and so did my mates

EXTRAS

This wasn't the only song that stole that Aussie tune. Dave 'Wooders' Woodley also wrote the following:

Once some jolly Pom fans
Sat beside a cricket field
Underneath the glare of the huge floodlights
And they sat and they sang
As they watched their team lose once again
We'll get pissed in St Kilda tonight

Pissed in St Kilda, pissed in St Kilda
We'll get pissed in St Kilda tonight
'Cos we're on a losing run
But you just can't keep our spirits down
We'll get pissed in St Kilda tonight

'YOU CAN SING SOD ALL'

This is the only song we know of that has had the direct input of an England player. This reworking of an Oasis classic was a collaboration between Barmy Army co-founder Paul Burnham and England all-rounder Dermot Reeve.

(to the tune of 'Wonderwall')

Today is gonna be the day that we're gonna sing a song
for you
By now you should've somehow realised that's what
we're here to do

And I don't believe that anybody sings as bad as you

Aussie Convicts

Backbeat, the word is on the street that you can't even
    write a song
I'm sure, you've heard it all before, but c'mon Aussies
    prove us wrong
'Cos I don't believe that anybody's quite as thick as you

Aussie Convicts

The 'Ooh aah' song you sing for Glenn is so sad
And 'Warney Warney Warney' is just as bad
There are many songs that I would like to hear from you
But you don't know how (don't know how)

'Cos maybe (maybe) you'll never find a song to play me
    (play me)
'Cos after all, you can sing sod all

'WE'VE BEEN TO ADELAIDE'

Doing an Ashes tour that includes Tasmania would be something of a rarity now and this song had already changed from its original incarnation (page 60). But this simple little ditty covering an Australian odyssey is still apt. It's a football song edited for cricketing purposes.

(to the tune of 'Those Were the Days')

We've been to Adelaide

We've been Tasmania

We've been to Perth

We've been to Brisbane too

We've been the MCG

We've been the SCG

And all because, oh England we love you

WHAT THEY SAY   BARMY  ARMY

'If I was given a chance to see just one more game, I wouldn't pick a game in England. I think I'd pick somewhere that was a lot more fun, all a little bit more light-hearted, all a little bit more raucous – let's say an Ashes Test in Sydney, where half the crowd are Barmy Army.'

— Barmy Army fan and occasional consultant, Dean Headley.

'TAKE THE URN HOME'

In the run-up to the 2010–11 Ashes series, there was a feeling among certain elements of the Barmy Army that we needed to update the songlist. The old anti-Aussie classics will always amuse, but some believed there was a need to rejuvenate the repertoire. Getting new songs off the ground is harder in Australia than anywhere else, but when Giles Wellington reworked the Beach Boys' classic 'Sloop John B' from the 2008 New Zealand tour (page 135), he was on to a winner.

(to the tune of 'Sloop John B')

We came over from old Blighty
The Barmy Army and me
Around Brisbane town we did roam

Six quid for a pint, a grand for a flight
With Strauss our captain, we'll take the urn home

(Chorus)
So hoist up the John B sail
See how the mainsail sails
Call for the captain ashore
Take the urn home
We'll take the urn home
We'll take the urn home
With Strauss our captain
We'll take the urn home

Ricky Ponting's a broken man
Without Warne he has no plan
He tries to carry the team all on his own
He's losing his hair
But we don't care
'Cos Strauss our captain will take the urn home

(Repeat Chorus)

Graeme Swann is a caring guy
Rescues cats in his spare time
Now he's gonna tear the Aussies apart
They can't read his spin

And so England will win
'Cos Strauss our captain will take the urn home
We'll take the urn home

(Repeat Chorus)

EXTRAS

Giles Wellington took his role so seriously he had singing lessons prior to the tour, much to the bemusement of his long-suffering wife Hayley, who was perplexed when her husband started walking round the house practising scales.

After the third Test of that series in Perth, the Barmy Army took a dislike to Brad Haddin for his excessive appealing and added a further verse:

Brad Haddin's a simple man
He appeals whenever he can
He even appeals a catch down the leg side (even a wide)
He's rubbish at his job
We think he's a knob
With Strauss our captain
We'll take the urn home

'YESTERDAY'

Going into that 2010–11 Ashes series determined to write new songs, the task was made easier for us by the obvious decline in the Australian side and the fact that they were missing their old superstars. That suggested a theme we could develop:

(to the tune of 'Yesterday')

Yesterday
Ponting's troubles seemed so far away
Now Nathan Hauritz is here to stay
McGrath and Warne were yesterday

Suddenly
They're not half the team they used to be
Will he lose Ashes number three
Yesterday came suddenly

Why Haydos
Had to go I don't know, Langer wouldn't say
Adam Gilchrist's gone, now Ricky longs for yesterday

EXTRAS

As it turned out, Nathan Hauritz wasn't here to stay – he didn't even get a game. But we soon found that there were plenty of others we could substitute.

THE ONE-LINERS

Sometimes you don't need a song, just a simple chant will pass on a message in no uncertain terms. These are just a few of the briefer options used by the Barmy Army:

We're the right side, we're the right side, we're the right side over here

We're the middle, we're the middle, we're the middle over here

We're the left side, we're the left side, we're the left side over here

You're the convicts, you're the convicts, you're the convicts over there

You're just a part of our empire, part of our empire

Get your shit stars off our flag

Captain Cook only stopped for a shit, doo-dah, doo-dah

You're just an English county

2 HEARD IT ALL BEFORE

NAME:
Paul Burnham

DAY JOB:
Barmy Army co-founder

How did Barmy Army singing evolve?

It began very much as a way of getting back at the Aussies for the grief we were copping from them. When we first started they were pretty abusive and, because we were losing so heavily, we didn't have much to throw back at them. Their heritage is an obvious target, which is why there are so many references to convicts, balls and chains, voting for the Queen and so on in our songs.

Although the Barmy Army is cricket-focused, there is obviously a crossover in terms of the fact that many cricket fans are also football fans. In the early days, many of the songs were football songs or reworked football songs. Although there are still some similarities, as many football and cricket songs are based on the same stock tunes, there's definitely been a move away from football chants over time.

The other big development was when we changed from singing songs about the Aussies to singing about our own players and really getting behind the team. In the early days, only a few players had songs written about them. And, if you look back at some of the early efforts for the players, there wasn't much in the way of sophistication about them. But, while the songs about Australia have stayed pretty much the same, the emphasis on writing songs for our own players is now huge.

Whenever a new player comes into the team, the usual songwriting suspects start colluding over a song for him. This was obvious in the recent tour of Sri Lanka when Samit Patel got into the team and we could sense that the England players were waiting to see what we came up with. His song hasn't made it into this book, as it isn't completely finished, but goes to the tune of 'Heartbeat':

> **Samit**
> **Samit Patel**
> **Why don't you take a wicket for me**
> **De de de de de de**

We're also a lot better at being topical now. If something happens then people can't help but start writing about it.

Where do you draw the line on what is acceptable in a song?
You have to react to the circumstances, as having blanket rules never works. Also, the Barmy Army can't dictate what people can and can't sing. We try to push the crowd in certain directions, but if they start singing something abusive then we don't really have the power to stop them. We can eject people if they are in Barmy Army-specific stands, and we can revoke memberships, but not everyone who joins in with the Barmy Army to sing some songs is an 'official' member.

The general guidelines I like to go by are simple. We prefer to keep swear words out of the songs as much as possible. The Barmy Army is for fans of all ages and all types, so singing something offensive is not really what we're about. A good example is the Jesse Ryder songs from the 2008 tour to New Zealand (page 135). The versions you see on YouTube have a sprinkling of mild swear words that we didn't replicate in the 'official' lyrics. But Doug, who wrote the songs, wasn't going to sing them like that, and given his audience over there why would he? Those songs work better with the swear words, but you just have to know the audience. Singing the same thing at a home Test match with a load of kids sat with us would be different.

We also try to make it more about supporting England than being abusive to opposition players. But at the same time it's always funny to write songs about our opponents, particularly when they are Australian. And while the majority of them are light-hearted piss-taking, we're probably more likely to push the boundaries for the Australian players because of the intensity of the rivalry.

The first South African tour the Barmy Army went on, in 1995–96, went too far when I look back now. We came up with chants that claimed Jonty Rhodes was a child molester, Paul Adams was a Thalidomide victim and Allan Donald was illegitimate. It was not only untrue, of course, but also I would now say that it wasn't funny, either. All those songs finished off with references to them being 'a Springbok bastard'. It was too much. I guess that was a result of the fact we hadn't completed the transition from football-style support to our own unique brand of backing. In football, opposition players can get fearful abuse, though even that is beginning to change nowadays.

How do you get new people involved in the singing?
We always need new recruits and it's great when you see new faces getting involved in the singing. It's probably easy for new people to get involved in Australia, where the songs are so ingrained with the regulars that people can pick them up easily. Conversely, that's the hardest time to get new songs going because there are so many people around.

We've printed songsheets, brought out magazines and now we've written this book to try to make it easy for people to know the words, but they have to meet us halfway and make an effort to learn the words. Everyone who has joined the Barmy Army has done it the same way, by picking up the song lyrics bit-by-bit, but our aim remains the same: we want more and more people singing as many different songs as possible.

What are your favourite songs?
My top three are the Simon Jones song (page 73), because it's just so clever with great cricket references and builds up to a great crescendo; Allan Donald (page 130), because it's the most fun and provided us with a lot of humour; and Deco's song (page 48), because it's also very clever and he is willing to stand up and sing it in front of everyone.

Best Barmy Army singing memory?
There have been so many, but the day we won the Test in Sydney on the 2002–03 tour was amazing. As usual, there were no

Aussies around to see it and we made so much noise in the ground, and then in the Captain Cook pub afterwards, it was awesome. What made that occasion so special was that we had nothing else to celebrate on the whole of that tour. By comparison, the Ashes in 2010–11 provided us with so many reasons to celebrate, so there was no one occasion that stood out in quite the same way.

3 ENGLAND PLAYERS – THE EARLY YEARS

In the early days of the Barmy Army, most of the songs were generic rather than aimed at particular individuals, but slowly the idea of writing player-specific songs did take hold, although the brevity of this chapter compared with later ones can be seen as a metaphor for the evolution of the Barmy Army. What started out as a way of fighting back against the Aussies only gradually became a way of supporting our own boys.

'ANGUS FRASER'

While Darren Gough was the first poster boy of the Barmy Army, Gus Fraser was revered and respected from day one. He was one of the first players to be serenaded with his own song.

His name is Super Gus Fraser

He's sharp as a razor

He bowls right-arm fast for England

When he walks down the street

All the people he meets

They say 'Hey! Big man!

What's your name?'

WHAT THEY SAY   BARMY ARMY

'As a player there was nothing better than hearing a section of the crowd you were playing in front of chanting your name. The reasons were twofold. The first was obvious: to receive such a response meant you had been or were performing well. The second was more subtle: if the supporters had bothered to produce a song with your name, it signified you meant something to them.'

— The man himself, Gus Fraser.

EXTRAS

Four years passed between Gus Fraser's last Test match and Steve Harmison's first. This song was in storage for that time, but was reworked for 'Super Steve Harmy' (see page 72).

'GOUGHIE THE KING'

Darren Gough was perhaps the first true Barmy Army hero. He managed to cover both bases by not only being one of the lads, a guy the Army would love to go for a beer with, but also by being extremely good at cricket. As the Aussies smashed us round the park, he was the big hope for the team and the one player who really took it to the Aussies.

(to the tune of 'Lily the Pink')
**We'll drink a drink a drink
To Goughie the king, the king, the king
He's the saviour of our cricket team
He is the greatest cricketer
That the world has ever seen**

WHAT THEY SAY   BARMY ✠ ARMY

'When he scores a Test fifty, he does not raise his bat in a self-justifying manner to his team-mates on the balcony, he twirls it round his head like a claymore for the benefit of the Barmy Army in the cheap seats.'

— Matthew Engel eulogising Gough after his Man of the Match performance in the third Test in 1995.

EXTRAS

Darren Gough is a big supporter of the Barmy Army Colts and his son Liam played for them.

'PHIL TUFNELL'

Phil Tufnell was another of the Army's early heroes and was also a renowned party animal. That reputation pretty much over-shadows memories of his cricketing ability for the Barmy Army, a fact reflected in his 'song'.

Phil Tufnell is having a party
Bring some drugs and a bottle of Bacardi
(Repeat ad infinitum)

WHAT THEY SAY   BARMY ARMY

'The MCG can be a bit of a lonely place when the Aussie batsmen are on top, so it's always nice to have a bit of your own stuff going on in the crowd.'

— Tuffers on the saving graces of the Army.

EXTRAS

Tuffers was never shy of enjoying a drink with the Army, and after the win in Adelaide on the 1994–95 tour, he stood on a table to lead a rousing rendition of 'If you've all shagged an Aussie clap your hands'.

'ANDY CADDICK'

Andy Caddick was born in New Zealand and as a result was the first recipient of a song based on coming from another country. He wouldn't be the last.

(to the tune of 'Oh, My Darling Clementine')

Andy Caddick, Andy Caddick
Must be worth five hundred grand
He was too good for New Zealand
So he plays for England

'NASSER HUSSAIN'

This was not necessarily the most sophisticated song we've ever come up with, but it made him happy and it wasn't exactly difficult for people to pick up.

(to the tune of 'Rupert the Bear')

Nasser, Nasser Hussain
Everyone knows his name
Nasser, Nasser Hussain
Everyone knows his name
It's Nasser Hussain!

WHAT THEY SAY

'In the mid-nineties, it frustrated Nasser Hussain that the Barmy Army had not created a song for him. When it eventually happened he was chuffed; it was as though he had finally made it as an England player.'

— Gus Fraser on exactly what it means to the players to have songs written in their honour.

EXTRAS

Nasser once signed an autograph for a fan with the sign-off: 'Everyone knows my name, Nasser Hussain.'

'ROBIN SMITH'

'Robin Hood' is a tune that is often at the forefront of people's minds when writing a song because it is catchy, simple and quintessentially English. When the player in question is called Robin to start with, it would seem churlish not to utilise it.

(to the tune of 'Robin Hood')
Robin Smith, Robin Smith
Willow in his hand
Robin Smith, Robin Smith
Feared throughout the land

Hits 'em for four, smacks 'em for six
Robin Smith, Robin Smith, Robin Smith

EXTRAS

Robin would go on to appear in the video for the ill-fated 'Come on England' single (page 144).

'PETER SUCH'

Whether they are one-Test wonders or players who had a long shelf life, spinners have always held a fascination for the Barmy Army. We have made pretty much every twirler into a cult hero, and among them was Peter Such – 'veteran' of 11 Test matches.

(to the tune of 'Another One Bites the Dust')

Da da do do do
There's only one Peter Such
Do do do
There's only one Peter Such

Oh
There's only one Pete
There's only one Pete
There's only one Peter Such

Hey, he's gonna get you too
There's only one Peter Such
Da da do do do

EXTRAS

Peter Such achieved the second longest duck in Test history at
51 balls. This had nothing to do with the Barmy Army, but we
had nothing else to write here and surely we should have written a song about it. 'And another dot ball and another dot ball,
another big duck for Such.'

'ALEX TUDOR'

Tenpole Tudor was a punk band fronted by Edward Tudor-
Pole. That's musical knowledge not shared by many, but
thankfully Gaz Taylor knew and so when Alex Tudor started his
Test career the song would be relevant, if not entirely prescient.

(to the tune of 'Swords of a Thousand Men')
He came to the WACA on a sunny day
He came from over 10,000 miles away
First he scored one
Then he scored four
Then he took Ponting, McGrath
And then Waugh Waugh Waugh

Say Tudor Tudor Tudaray

His name's Alex Tudor and he's gonna take your
stumps away

Der-der, Der-dup

Der-der, Der-dup

Der-der, Der-dup Der-der

Say Tudor Tudor Tudaray

His name's Alex Tudor and he's gonna take your
stumps away

EXTRAS

Tudor once made England fans boo one of his team-mates. As a nightwatchman, he scored 99 not out and fans booed batting partner Graham Thorpe for leaving him stranded.

I WRITE THE SONGS

NAME:
Dave Woodley, aka Wooders

DAY JOB:
Quantity Surveyor

What is the key to writing a successful song?
If by successful you mean one that will be regularly sung on the terraces by the Barmy Army, then I think that you really have to be looking at keeping things brief. It's very difficult for a large group of people to keep in time and in tune to an epic, which is part of the reason why many of the songs I've written didn't really make it to the terraces.

Picking the right song to base your new lyrics on is also important. It's not just about finding a good tune that everyone knows; it works best when you've picked a song that also has the right kind of spirit to suit your new lyrics. If you're really good, then you manage to ride the zeitgeist and stick some new lyrics to the major song of the moment, which everyone will know.

One particular song I remember, not that I wrote it, was during the West Indies tour of 1998, where we ended up playing two Tests in Trinidad because of the abandoned Test in Jamaica. We lost the first one in Trinidad but won the second, so all the fans were happy to be leaving Trinidad with the series even. At that time a major song in England was 'Tubthumping' by Chumbawumba, ideal material with a chanting-style chorus that anybody could sing along to, even after a few beers, so someone had picked up on that and gave us the very simple but very effective 'We went one down, but we got up again, you ain't never gonna keep us down'.

What was the first song you came up with?
That would be my Steve Bucknor song, written to the tune of 'Delilah' during the Melbourne Test of Christmas 1994. It was my first overseas Test with England and my first with the Barmy Army. They'd been singing 'Delilah' a lot, because one of the key characters in the Army was a lad called McGiff from Stoke and he'd sung it when watching Stoke City, where the fans had adopted it.

Mike Atherton had been getting what seemed to us to be some pretty rough treatment from the umpires, and in the second innings he was given out caught behind by Steve Bucknor. From where we were sitting in the stands, most of us were pretty certain that he hadn't got an edge on it. So I came up with some lyrics about the situation and 'Delilah' seemed like a good choice, because the boys had all been singing it anyway. I got hold of some movie posters from a local video shop and wrote the lyrics on the back with a marker, so that they would be big enough for people to read for at least a few rows, and it was debuted in the Royal Hotel, Richmond, after the next day's play. It went:

> I saw the gap 'tween the ball and the bat as it flew by
> You didn't so you gave Mike out, that's when I started
>   to cry
> He never touched it
> But you raised your finger and Mike was out wrongly
>   once more
>
> Why, why, why, Steve Bucknor
> You lie, lie, lie, Steve Bucknor
> And so, before we come to break down your door
> Forgive us Steve Bucknor
> We're not gonna take any more

What is the best song you've written?
It's very difficult to be objective and say which of my own songs is the best, it's like trying to be objective about your children; you always think they're far cuter and more intelligent than the other kids in their class. If I apply my own criteria about what makes a good song then I guess the one that best fits was the Andy

Caddick song (page 25) that I wrote during the tour to the Windies in 1998. It was brief and to the point, easy to remember and was written in the space of a couple of hours.

What is your favourite song that's not yours?

It has to be the Mitchell Johnson song (page 92), which as of today seems to have finished his Test career. Again, it's brief and easy to remember and has a nice sedate tempo which really allows everyone singing to give it their all. Mitchell made the mistake of admitting that the fans got under his skin during the 2009 series, so whoever wrote this one knew his target was vulnerable.

What is your best Barmy Army singing memory?

After winning the Adelaide Test in 1995, the Army retired to our regular pub for that week, the Lord Raglan, to celebrate. During the course of the evening most of the touring party stopped by, some staying longer than others. At one point the whole pub was singing 'Who ate all the pies?' at the tops of their voices. And, in the middle of the pub, with the most enormous grin on his face, stood Mike Gatting, arms raised in the air, wrists cocked and index fingers pointing straight at his ample paunch. Off the back of that win in Adelaide I wrote another song based on 'Delilah':

I saw the catch of the match by Tufnell off Slater
Boon for no score.
Then Steve Waugh not very much later

34

He lost his off stump

We won the Test match and went down the pub for the
     night

Bye, bye, bye Australia

It was time we nailed ya

And so, before we come to Perth for the draw

Admit it Australia

You're not going to win any more

Sadly, that proved to be a case of undue optimism.

BARMY ARMY

4 THE BARMY ARMY STANDARDS

This is a motley collection of classic songs of patriotism, nonsensical ramblings of which Edward Lear would have been proud, the Barmy Army's signature tune, and classic ditties that work well any time, any place and anywhere. Perhaps we should have called this the Martini chapter ...

'JERUSALEM'

'Jerusalem' is the preferred 'national' anthem for the Barmy Army, and there is a feeling among the troops that this is England's song rather than Britain's. It is now an integral part of any day at Test cricket and is specifically sung at the start of play.

And did those feet in ancient time
Walk upon England's mountains green?
And was the holy Lamb of God
On England's pleasant pastures seen?

And did the Countenance Divine
Shine forth upon our clouded hills?
And was Jerusalem builded here
Among those dark Satanic mills?

Bring me my bow of burning gold
Bring me my arrows of desire
Bring me my spear: O clouds unfold!
Bring me my chariot of fire

I will not cease from mental fight
Nor shall my sword sleep in my hand
Till we have built Jerusalem
In England's green and pleasant land

WHAT THEY SAY

BARMY ARMY

'It is my favourite song, and if you get a whole load of people singing it, it's incredibly powerful. But when I get the fifth pissed-up bloke in a row coming up to me and wanting me to play "Jerusalem" it can get a bit monotonous.'

— Billy 'the Trumpet' Cooper.

'Worst of all, the England and Wales Cricket Board have fallen in with this travesty of the spirit of cricket, having adopted the Barmy Army's habit of singing – or rather yelling – "Jerusalem" at the beginning of each day's play of a Test match.'

— Dominic Lawson, who is not exactly an advocate of the Barmy Army. But then we're not in his fan club either.

EXTRAS

Singing the song is one thing. Doing the hand movements is another. 'Bring me my bow' should be sung pulling back an imaginary longbow. 'Bring me my arrows' with some imaginary dart-throwing. Clouds are unfolded with extravagant waving gestures and the chariots of fire are horse-drawn in our imaginary world. Mental fight is not ceased with a tap to the head, before finally an imaginary sword is drawn that will never sleep in our hands.

'RULE BRITANNIA'

This is another song that has absolutely nothing to do with the songwriting abilities of the Barmy Army, but it cannot be left out of this tome. In truth, the majority of people don't even know the words. One man who does is Graham Barber, aka Big G or Norfolk Graham, whose falsetto voice has made him famous in cricket grounds around the world. A few join him in singing the verse, but everyone joins in the chorus. Debate rages about whether this is an apt song to sing, particularly in the Caribbean, but to us it's just another patriotic anthem that we love to sing.

When Britain first, at Heaven's command
Arose from out the azure main
Arose from, arose from out the azure main
This was the charter, the charter of the Land
And Guardian Angels sang this strain

Rule Britannia, Britannia rule the waves!
Britons never, ever, ever shall be slaves
Rule Britannia, Britannia rule the waves!
Britons never, ever, ever shall be slaves

WHAT THEY SAY

'Getting Norfolk Graham to sing "Rule Britannia" for us was awesome. I think there are times when we want to join in the songs when we are out on the field, but it probably wouldn't go down well with the management, so it was nice to be able to belt something out.'

— Matthew Hoggard, after the England players came over to the fans while celebrating the 2008 series win over New Zealand.

'SONG FOR JIMMY SAVILE'

Vic Flowers, aka Jimmy Savile, is the figurehead for the Barmy Army and is famed for his 'one song'. It was during the South Africa series 1999–2000 that he made 'Everywhere We Go' his own, and this tune was written subsequently as a way of introducing the following rendition of the classic.

(to the tune of 'Jim'll Fix It')
He came to South Africa
And that was the start of it
He drank with the Army
And now he's a part of it
Now then, now then
Jim'll fix it for you
And you and you and ba ba ba

WHAT THEY SAY

BARMY ![flag] **ARMY**

'I went to see my first Test match in Melbourne 1998. I'd never heard of the Barmy Army before that. As soon as I saw and heard it in action, I thought, "This is all right." But I never, ever thought it would progress to where it is at now. The next tour was for the millennium in South Africa, and I bought a silly hat with "Millennium" written on it. I was already wearing the singlet and they seemed to go together.'

— Vic Flowers on how he metamorphosed into Jimmy Savile.

'EVERYWHERE WE GO'

'Everywhere We Go' is a song that has been utilised by a wide variety of groups from scouts and guides to sports fans of differing persuasions. It doesn't belong to any of them, but within the cricketing fraternity there is certainly a feeling that the Barmy Army has now adopted it as its own. It's the most popular song for newcomers, as it is the easiest to join in and the one that makes people feel like they are a part of the Army. And for the captain of the England cricket team at any given time, it reminds them that the Barmy Army belongs to them. Jimmy will sing one line, and then the crowd will echo it back to him. Because of that, most people take their first tentative steps into the Barmy Army world with this song.

Jimmy: Everywhere we go

Crowd: Everywhere we go

The people want to know

Who we are

Where we come from

Shall we tell them

Who we are

Where we come from

We are the England

The mighty mighty England

We are the Army

The Barmy Barmy Army

Andrew Strauss's Barmy Army

(repeat)

WHAT THEY SAY

'One of the saddest moments in my career was when it went from being "Nasser Hussain's Barmy Army" to "Michael Vaughan's Barmy Army" ... There was nothing better than hearing them singing that.'

— Nasser Hussain on his sadness at handing over his army to a new leader.

'I'd heard "Everywhere We Go" being sung, so I had a go at leading it. I kept getting the words wrong though.'

— Vic struggled in his new role to start with, and it didn't go unnoticed ...

'You're doing a great job, but it would be good if you could learn the right words.'

— Whether it was too much beer, sunstroke or just a lack of concentration that caused Vic to fluff his lines, Barmy Army co-founder Paul Burnham still remained supportive.

'Close analysis of the text seems futile.'

— Journalist Matthew Norman, before going on to analyse the text in his *Daily Telegraph* column. His analysis might have been vaguely relevant if he'd actually got the lyrics right. Perhaps he had consulted with Jimmy.

EXTRAS

When the song goes on for a long time, we have been known to mix it up by using other ex-England captains' and players' names such as Nasser Hussain, David Gower, Ian Botham and as far back as Douglas Jardine to really wind up the Australians. On occasions, we have been known to stand on one leg singing 'On one leg, Barmy Army' and other random variations.

'WE ARE THE ARMY'

'We Are the Army' is very much a football song that was an obvious translation to cricket. And while every football team in the world might claim to have the most loyal football supporters, there's not much real doubt that we're the most loyal cricket fans.

(to the tune of 'You Are My Sunshine')

We are the Army, the Barmy Army
Oh we are mental, and we are mad
We are the loyalest cricket supporters
That the world has ever had

WHAT THEY SAY

'I soon realised they weren't fickle, they weren't just there to support us when things were going well and then go quiet and moody when they weren't ... You could set your watch by them. They would kick off with the usual tunes and you'd turn round to the lads and say "The Barmy Army are awake, let's get going boys." It became a regular part of our day.'

— Nasser Hussain remembers the reliability of the Army.

EXTRAS

We often argue about the words of a song, but it's not often the spelling and grammar cause issues. 'Loyalest' should really be 'most loyal', but that would not fit the rhythm of the song. Some, therefore, wanted to spell it 'loyalist', but we didn't want it to have political connotations. So 'loyalest' it remains.

'WE ARE THE BARMY BOYS'

Another tune that is more reflective of the days when football chants were translated to the cricketing arena, this catchy little number is fairly sensible for the first, repeated verse, and wonderfully nonsensical for the last. The reference to not filling a fridge is relevant, as most countries struggle to attract crowds to Test matches, but as for the rest . . . who knows?

(to the tune of 'Marching Through Georgia')
I-oh, I-oh
We are the Barmy boys
I-oh, I-oh
We are the Barmy boys
We're England's famous cricket fans
We travel near and far
When we're not singing
You'll find us at the bar

(Repeat verse one)

I-oh, I-oh
You couldn't fill a fridge
I-oh, I-oh
You couldn't fill a fridge
Your mother's wearing Tupperware
Your father's wearing pants
We're all going to a disco dance

WHAT THEY SAY

'I reckon the Barmy Army create a great atmosphere, and a uniquely English atmosphere. At overseas Tests, they help fill stadiums and they have a good economic impact.'

— Matthew Hayden has noticed that the 'singing' bit creates an atmosphere, and he's right that the 'find us at the bar' part is pretty good for the economy as well.

'WHEN I WAS SIX'

The previous two songs were pretty straight translations from football to cricket. And indeed this one is another that has its roots in football, but we decided to change it. Certain football clubs' fans give it a pay-off line that says 'F*** the Pope and the IRA', but our version is about love, not hate.

When I was six, I had no sense
I bought a flute for fifty pence
The only tune that I could play
Was Andrew Strauss's Barmy Army

EXTRAS

Trying to research the origins of this song, we came across this old US folk version:

When I was little, I had no sense
I took a whiz on the electric fence
It hurt so bad, it burned my balls
And then I took a poop in my overalls

'DECO'S SONG'

Deco has become a Barmy Army icon, famous for the singing of this song and for his intense love of Matthew Prior that has inspired him to write a litany of tunes for the love of his life. When KP asked him why he was called Deco, he was surprised that there was any confusion. After he explained that it was because he was a decorator, KP employed him to do up his house. But it is this song, and not his painting skills, that brought him to prominence.

(to the tune of 'Lord of the Dance')

We sang in the morning at the start of the Test
We sang up to lunch then we went and had a rest
We came back from lunch then we sang till tea
It's fun being in the Barmy Army

(Chorus)
Sing sing wherever you may be
We are the famous Barmy Army
And we'll cheer England on wherever they may be
And we'll sing them on to another victory

Now an Ashes summer makes us all so proud
It's fun watching England hit the convicts round the
    ground
We'll sing for our batsmen and our bowlers too
'Cos they make all our dreams come true

(Repeat Chorus)

Now our ticket prices don't seem to be fair
But look at our faces, do you think we even care?
We've come in our numbers and we're gonna see
Another famous Ashes victory

(Repeat Chorus)

At the end of this song, I hope the message is clear

We are the fans that will always come and cheer

So thanks everybody for singing with me

'Cos we're all part of the Barmy Army

(Repeat Chorus)

WHAT THEY SAY

'I wrote the song after the funeral of a friend of mine, as she loved "Lord of the Dance" and I thought it would be a lasting tribute to her. I wrote it during the summer of 2006 and I first sang it in the West End bar in Mumbai after we won a Test match in India for the first time in 26 years. Then Paul Burnham urged me to enter it in a song competition judged by Stephen Fry to get a free, all-inclusive trip to Melbourne and Sydney for the 2006–07 Ashes series. It came second to 'Hey, Hey We're the Barmies' – that well-known Barmy Army song!

'I never really sang it much in Oz, but in New Zealand 2008 it became a big hit with the boys and really the rest is history. There have been lots of special times singing it, but barring singing it to Matty [Prior] and the boys after our win in Durban on the South Africa 2009–10 tour, it really felt the best singing it on the last Ashes tour. As the song is celebrating the Barmy Army's loyal support for our England cricketing heroes and it also has a pop at the convicts, there's nothing better than giving it to the convicts in their own backyard.

'If I had to nail one particular time, then it would have to be the last day at Sydney on the 2010–11 Ashes tour. England were cruising to a three-one victory and singing it that morning meant the world to me, not just because England had won the Ashes, but for the memory of my friend … We'd done it!'

— Deco explains how Barmy Army songs can sometimes transcend the cricket.

EXTRAS

Deco's reference to the 'well-known Barmy Army song' is laced with sarcasm, as it never took off in the grounds and might never have made it into this book if it wasn't for Deco's reference. But here are the lyrics anyway so you can judge for yourself.

'HEY, HEY WE'RE THE BARMIES'

(to the tune of 'The Monkees')

Here we come
Walkin' down your beach
Get admiring looks from
All the sheilas we meet

Hey, hey we're the Barmies
And people say we're vulgar and loud
But we're too busy singing
To put anybody down

We'll go to the Gabba in Brisbane
And the Waca in Perth
We won't have time to be thirsty
Swimming in beer and mirth

Hey, hey we're the Barmies
And people say we're barmy and proud
But we're too busy drinking
To put anybody down

We're just trying to be friendly
Come and watch us sing and play

We're the Mighty England
And we've got plenty to say

You're just trying to be nasty
We've come to watch our team play
You're bad losers and convicts
And you've got nothing to say

Hey, hey we're the Barmies
All colour, excitement and sound
So you'd all better be ready
We've come to take over your ground

'TAKE ME HOME'

John Denver's classic has been a regular for as long as most Barmies can remember, but over the last couple of years it has taken on a new lease of life and become a favourite for many. This has little to do with the song itself and more to do with the juvenile behaviour that sees us vary the pace from drawn-out renditions, where each word is held as long as our breaths last, to ridiculously quick versions where we can barely get the words out quick enough to keep up with Bill's trumpeting. The lyrics are interchangeable depending on the particular series. But here is one version:

Take me home
Andrew Strauss
To the place I belong
Three-one series, Ashes trophy
Take me home, Andrew Strauss

EXTRAS

We incurred the wrath of the National Bank during the 2008 New Zealand tour. The National Bank used to belong to the Lloyds Bank group and utilises the same black horse logo. When we sang 'Lloyds Bank trophy', a marketing dude asked if we could sing the proper name of the bank. If they had turned up with a crate of beer we'd probably have done it, but we roll over for corporates only if there's something in it for us.

'WE ARE ENGLAND'

A simple football tune conversion that made it from football to cricket.

E-I-E-I-E-I-O
Off to Melbourne we will go
When we win the Ashes
This is what we'll sing

We are England
We are England
Straussy is our King

'IN THE JUNGLE'

Graham Barber's alternative party piece (other than 'Rule Britannia' on page 40) is this classic that works so well because his voice carries a long way and acts as a call to arms for the singing masses. The chorus is easy and repeatable, and it has the additional advantage that it is also adaptable to different tours and drinks. We've chosen this particular version because Kandy is as near to the jungle as we get, and Lion (that sleeps tonight) is our beer of choice in Sri Lanka.

(to the tune of 'The Lion Sleeps Tonight')
Dee do dee do
De de doo de doo
Eee um Wimoweh

In the jungle

The Kandy jungle

It's Lion beer tonight

In the jungle

The Kandy jungle

It's Lion beer tonight

We'll win away, we'll win away

WHAT THEY SAY   BARMY   ARMY

'Where is the dude from the Barmy Army who sings "In the Jungle"?!?! He'd win this *Voice* thing hands down!!'

— Stuart Broad tweeting for Big G to hit the small screen.

EXTRAS

This song is a great advert for our favourite beers in whatever country we happen to be in. Other drinks to have been mentioned include Rum and Ting (Ting being a soft drink in the Caribbean), Jagerbombs (a Barmy Army staple) and Monkbombs (a drink we have in India where they have no Jagermeister, so we replace it with Old Monk rum).

Big G is no shrinking violet, but can sometimes take some

cajoling to sing the song. During the second Test in Mohali 2008 there was an outside influence, however, as Kingfisher is not only the name of our beer of choice, but also a domestic airline. Every time a Kingfisher plane appeared overhead, we belted out the chorus and he had little choice but to do the rest.

Paul Collingwood has been heard several times trying to replicate Graham's party piece. He's not bad, but although he has now given up the Test cricket day job we recommend that singing is not in his retirement plan.

'WHEN THIS BLOODY TOUR IS OVER'

This is a variation on an old war song called 'When this Bloody War is Over' that was introduced to the Barmy Army by the legendary Jack Hyams. He was 79 when he joined in the cricketing army, as opposed to the real one. Sadly, Jack passed away while this book was being written.

(to the tune of 'What a Friend We Have in Jesus')

When this bloody tour is over
Oh how happy I will be
On the plane home back to England
No more Aussie cheats for me
No more cheating Aussie umpires
No more catches off the grass

We can tell those cheating Aussies
To stick our Ashes up their arse

EXTRAS

It's another song that is rarely sung the same way twice, as it's easily customisable for each tour. During the recent tour of Sri Lanka when the Sri Lankan Cricket Board (led by Arjuna Ranatunga) decided to charge £25 a day for tickets, we decided to change the final two lines to: 'We will tell that bloody Ranatunga/To shove his tickets up his arse'.

I WRITE THE SONGS

NAME:
Gary Taylor aka Gaz

DAY JOB:
Company Director,
British Sports Museum.com

What is the key to writing a successful song?

Find a tune everyone knows and loves, ideally a terrace anthem. You can identify a popular terrace anthem by the fact that most (football) teams around the country will sing it, but everyone has different words. The second point will be to keep the lyrics simple; sometimes you can be clear in the verse and given a bit of choir practice in the pub you'll find a few that will remember the words, but the chorus must be simple and memorable for everyone, as most times when they are called on to sing it they will be 'three sheets to the wind' and memory won't be a strong point.

First song you came up with?

It was way too long ago to remember. 'The Aussies Love the English' (page 4) was one of the earlier ones, but definitely not the first.

Best song you've written?

Probably 'Shane Warne's Villa' (page 89). I wrote it during the 2005 Ashes when I was imagining us winning the Ashes at The Oval and everyone singing it as we lifted the Urn. At the time it seemed an impossible dream, but one that came true.

Favourite song that's not yours?

The original version of 'We've Been to Adelaide', that went:

(to the tune of 'Those Were The Days')

We've been to Adelaide
We've been Ballarat
We've been to Perth
We've been to Albury too
We've been the SCG
We've been the MCG and all because
Oh England we love you

Best Barmy Army singing memory?

We were driving across the Nullarbor following the Perth Test on our way to Adelaide and we had two or three days of nothing, no newspapers and no shops. As we finally came into the first town in South Australia there was a newsagent with a board outside proclaiming 'Aussie Captain in Bribe Shocker'. We bought the paper and were amazed to find out that Waugh and Warne were at the centre of bribe allegations from a previous tour and the whole thing had apparently been covered up by the ACB. During the drive down to Adelaide I started writing a song about the story. I was trying each line out on Big John and Tony Farrell, who were sitting in the back of the car. By the time we got to Adelaide I had 'Mark Waugh is an Aussie' (see page 82).

When I met up with the rest of the Barmy Army, the song just took off. We had a Barmy Army night at the Adelaide jail a few nights later, there were news crews there and we sang the song and before I knew it the thing was being broadcast across Australia on the news, with the lyrics subtitled on the bottom of the screen.

But the thing I remember the most was long after the Test series ended. In the final ODI in the World Series we [the remaining members of the Barmy Army] decided to sit up in the gods away from the main section of English. As I watched 6,000 English sing that song, it was a bizarre feeling.

5 ENGLAND PLAYERS – THE 2005 ASHES WINNERS

In an attempt to split up the songs about England players we've drawn some arbitrary lines, but this group of players was around for one of the great moments in English cricket and many of them were long-term Barmy Army heroes, so it seemed a good grouping. KP isn't here because his songs were written later – all these were sung during that epic series.

'MICHAEL VAUGHAN MY LORD'

It may seem simplistic, but the reverence in which Vaughan was held, especially after his stunning 2002–03 Ashes series, made this song particularly apt. It would generally be accompanied with a mass bowing in his direction, of the type more often seen in reverence to a deity, or perhaps Kim Jong-il before he went to the dictatorship in the sky.

(to the tune of 'Kumbaya')
Michael Vaughan my Lord, Michael Vaughan
Michael Vaughan my Lord, Michael Vaughan
Michael Vaughan my Lord, Michael Vaughan
Ohh Lord Michael Vaughan

EXTRAS

Our love for Michael Vaughan was reciprocated. During a post-series session with most of the squad in New Zealand 2008, he made a request for us to start singing again and our response was along the lines of 'If you want us to sing again, why don't you start a song?' For a man who faced up to 90mph bowling without fear he looked terrified, but as everyone in the bar chanted 'Vaughney gi's a song' he had no choice and with a little prompting kicked off a tune. Having done his bit, he was quick to drop his team-mates in it and ensure they all had to start one as well.

'TRESCOTHICK, SUPERSTAR'

If you want statistical accuracy this one is not for you, so pedants can stop here. Comparisons with two of the greatest batsmen of all time showed the regard in which we held Tresco.

(to the tune of 'Jesus Christ Superstar')

Trescothick, Superstar
Scores more runs than Tendulkar
Trescothick, Superstar
Scores more runs than Brian Lara

EXTRAS

Ravi Bopara had a similar song written about him to the tune of 'Radio Ga-Ga' that insisted he was 'better than Lara and Sangakkara'. Sadly for Ravi, that one never took off in the same way. Maybe there's still time . . .

'STRAUSS, STRAUSS, NEVER GETS OUT'

There are some songs that have a horribly fatalistic element to them. If you include the line 'Never gets out' in a song, you'd better make sure you don't sing it as he gets out otherwise you feel mighty stupid. And many in the Barmy Army believe strongly in the power of the jinx.

(to the tune of Tears For Fears' 'Shout')

Strauss, Strauss

Never gets out

He plays the shots that we dream about

Come on, we're talking 'bout you

Come on

EXTRAS

Andrew's wife Ruth once made a request to come and sing 'Jerusalem' with the Barmy Army because she loves us so much. Sadly, we never quite got round to facilitating it, but she did always make a point of appreciating our support.

'ANDREW FLINTOFF'

Like Darren Gough, Andrew Flintoff was a Boy's Own character who embodied what the Barmy Army wanted in a cricketer – a drinker with a bit of attitude and a sprinkling of genius. This song was another that induced big crowd participation because it was a follow-my-leader effort, so knowledge of the words was unimportant. And because the song built up line-by-line, the volume would invariably increase as it went on. The leader was usually Neil Rowe, aka Southgate, who was often seen in the ground dressed as HM The Queen.

(to the tune of 'Alouette')

Southgate: Oh how we love

Crowd: Oh how we love

Our all-round man (our all-round man)

Oh . . . Freddie Flintoff, Freddie Freddie Flintoff

Freddie Flintoff, Freddie Freddie Flintoff

Oh how we love (Oh how we love)

Your six hitting (your six hitting)

Our all-round man (our all-round man)

Oh . . . Freddie Flintoff, Freddie Freddie Flintoff

Freddie Flintoff, Freddie Freddie Flintoff

(And so on until the final verse)

Your pedalo

Your gorgeous wife

Your ample girth

Your chain smoking

Your beer drinking

Your slip catching

Your seam bowling

Your six hitting

Our all-round man

EXTRAS

Back in the days of Freddie's pomp, there were a couple of Barmy Army types who used to dress up as the Pink Panther and Sylvester the Cat. Flintoff once borrowed the Sylvester costume, joined up with the rest of the team and started playing the fool. It took his mates an hour to realise it was him and not a fan.

'THE MATTHEW HOGGARD SONG'

Hoggy's first song was the same as Flintoff's in terms of structure, but with different attributes.

Oh how we love

Your twelve wickets

Our nightwatchman

Our hat-trick boy (Sarwan, Hines and Chanderpaul!)

Your straight batting

Your swing bowling

Your pigeon-toes
Your knobbly knees
Your smelly farts
Your loping gait
Your two-cross eyes
Your straggly hair
Your floppy hat
Our Yorkshire boy
Oh . . . Matty Hoggard, Matty, Matty Hoggard
Matty Hoggard, Matty, Matty Hoggard

WHAT THEY SAY

'It's a great feeling going down to fine leg and having people sing about you and having your own song, especially if you're not feeling great or struggling a bit in the field – it's great to have people backing you.'

— Matthew Hoggard explains to the Barmy Army how they can cheer him up.

'And they sing some very nice songs about me. I found that a bit weird at first, but I soon got used to it.'

— More words of Hoggard.

'KING OF THE SWINGERS'

If ever there was an England cricketer who would have been at home as a member of the animal kingdom it was wannabe veterinarian Matthew Hoggard, so the choice of song was very apt.

(to the tune of 'I Wan'na Be Like You')

Now Hoggy's the king of the swingers

An England VIP

He has a bowl, the wickets roll

The convicts out by tea

Oohh Oohh Oohh,

I wanna bowl like you-ou-ou

Don't wanna bat like you, just bowl like you do-o-o

Oh yeah it's true-ue-ue

I wanna bowl like you-ou-ou

Don't wanna bat like you, just bowl like you-ou-ou.

WHAT THEY SAY

'A bit harsh about the batting, perhaps, but I can forgive them that much. And I would usually respond with a monkey impression, which only seemed fair.'

— Hoggard loved to play up to the Barmy Army.

'ASHLEY GILES'

Giles picked up the nickname 'King of Spain' when a batch of mugs celebrating the spinner was mistakenly inscribed with that moniker as opposed to 'King of Spin'. The mugs are now collectors' items and Warwickshire even went so far as to print more mugs with Giles on one side and King Juan Carlos of Spain on the other. Easy meat for the songwriting fraternity.

(to the tune of 'Give Me Joy')
Give me joy in my heart, keep it spinning
Give me joy in my heart I pray
Give me joy in my heart, keep it spinning
Keep it spinning 'til the close of play

Ashley Giles, Ashley Giles
Ashley Giles is the King of Spain

Ashley Giles, Ashley Giles
Ashley Giles is the King of Spain

Juan Carlos, Juan Carlos
Juan Carlos is the King of spin

'SUPER STEVE HARMY'

There is a general tendency to avoid merely reworking an old player's song to a new one, but Gus Fraser's seemed to fit Steve Harmison so well it quickly became his.

My name is Super Steve Harmy
They all think I'm barmy
I bowl right arm fast for England
When I walk down the street
All the people I meet
They say Hey! Big man!
What's your name?

EXTRAS

During the 2007 tour to Sri Lanka, Harmy was in need of support. We gave it to him by singing this incessantly on one particular day, which was fine except some of us couldn't sleep that night as it continued to buzz around our booze-addled brains.

'SIMON JONES'

Ask any of the Barmy Army who have been around for a few years for their favourite song and this will usually get a mention. The fact that Simon Jones is Welsh makes 'Men of Harlech' ideal. The quality of the songwriting, considering the difficulty of the tune, is exemplary.

(to the tune of 'Men of Harlech')
Men of England do not fear
We have brought a bowler here
Who has batsman far and near
Shaken to the bone

Ricky Ponting stop your dreaming
We can see the new ball gleaming
See it swinging, see it seaming
Bring on Simon Jones

Aussie wickets falling
Makes them look appalling
Bring on Simon Jones

You hear the Barmy Army calling
He has pace and he has power
See those Aussie batsmen cower
Ninety-nine miles an hour
Bring on Simon Jones

EXTRAS

During the 2009 Ashes series first Test in Cardiff, Simon Jones showed his appreciation for the Army by joining us in the stands for a while. He looked suitably embarrassed as we serenaded him with this song.

'DRINK WITH THE ARMY'

Chaz, the writer of this song and interviewee in this book, says it was based on the theme tune of a 1960s/70s TV sitcom called *When the Boat Comes In.* He doesn't look old enough to have been watching it then, so we're not sure how it got into his consciousness, but a bit of research reveals it's actually an old English folk song that originated in Northumberland, which is nice as that's in the same neck of the woods as Colly's County Durham birthplace.

(to the tune of 'When the Boat Comes In')
Who will take his wicket
Spinners he will pick it

Never take his wicket
When Collingwood comes in

Drink with the Army
Sing with the Army
Drink with the Army
When Collingwood comes in

Drink with the Army
Sing with the Army
Drink with the Army
Sing with the Army
Drink with the Army
When Collingwood comes in

EXTRAS

Most Barmy Army songs are reactive, but this one was actually predictive. Paul Collingwood has vowed to join the Barmy Army in the stands once his cricketing career has ended, so he really will 'drink with the Army, sing with the Army'.

'GERAINT JONES'

Born in Papua New Guinea of Welsh parents, but raised in Australia, Geraint Jones was about as English as boomerangs.

But like Andrew Caddick before him, that merely gave the Barmy Army songwriters something easy to work with.

(to the tune of 'Oh, My Darling Clementine')

Geraint Jonesy, Geraint Jonesy

Must be worth five hundred grand

He was too good for the convicts

So he plays for England

EXTRAS

Jones made an international comeback in 2012 . . . playing for Papua New Guinea. We wonder if the PNG Barmy Army have changed this song to 'He was too good for the England, so he plays for PNG'. No, thought not.

I WRITE
THE SONGS

3

NAME:
Gaz Fulton and Dave 'Spooner'
Fradley aka Chaz and Dave

DAY JOB:
Local Government Officer/
Business Analyst

What is the key to writing a successful song?

Chaz: It depends what type you're writing. The general England
ones need to be short and easy to learn, but the ones for the
players can be a bit more complex. It also helps to get a bit of
humour in there, but many are adapted from songs from other
sports. A lot now are churned out by the Barmy Army think tank –
a collective effort – when a new player comes into the side and
needs a song. Some great ones have come from this as in the Ally
Cook (page 98) and Paul Collingwood (page 74) numbers. The best
songs seem to be written when you are in obscure Test match
venues like Dhaka or Nagpur when there are fewer supporters
there. It's easier to get the song going then.

Dave: Just like Ian Bell you have got to have a hook that's going to stick in people's minds. Mix in muchos booze and the verses look after themselves; just make sure someone is on hand to record the composition.

First song you came up with?

Chaz: It wasn't quite 'Snooker Loopy', but I think it was 'When I was Six' (page 47) in Melbourne 1998. It's a classic that still gets churned out now, you just put in your different captain. Alec Stewart was that man on our first tour and I remember the Army acquiring the sign from the scoreboard in a warm-up game in Cairns with 'A Stewart' on and that was carried around for the whole tour and can be seen on many crowd photos from that series.

Best song you've written?

Chaz: 'We Are the Army' (page 45), although some people won't thank me for that. It can go on a bit, to be fair. I reckon it's a good one to drop in and stop 'Everywhere We Go' going on for ever.

Favourite song that's not yours?

Chaz: I love a song that gets a player's reaction and they show appreciation for the support. So I'd have to say 'He's Matty Prior' (page 114), 'Swanny Super Over' (page 110) or the Sidebottom ones (page 101).

Dave: Gilo's 'Take the Urn Home' (page 10) or Hoggy's 'King of the Swingers' (page 70). 'The Dog Called Prince' song is actually written by Nigel Blackwell of Half Man Half Biscuit and is called 'Paintball's Coming Home' – classic. (NB – we haven't provided the lyrics to this because they aren't ours to print. But we suggest you take a look at YouTube for 'Paintball's Coming Home', rejoice in its randomness and appreciate why we love it.)

Best Barmy Army singing memory?

Chaz: A strip club in Adelaide in 1998 where the act came out to 'Another One Bites the Dust' and the whole room burst into 'There's Only One Peter Such. Oh he's gonna get you too!'

Dave: Memories? What are they?

6 AUSTRALIAN PLAYERS

BARMY ARMY

The Barmy Army is primarily about supporting England and there is an effort to ensure that any songs about the opposition are banter rather than abuse. With the Aussies we push the barriers, but they are such obvious targets and often leave themselves wide open for a bit of good-natured ribbing.

We're not really sure why so many of these songs are to the tune of 'My Old Man's a Dustman', but it's the most-utilised Barmy Army song overall. Maybe it's because it's simplistic, catchy and easy to rework and songwriters admit that when they try to write a new song an old one often creeps into the brain without being beckoned.

'MARK WAUGH IS AN AUSSIE'

Prior to the third Test of the 1998–99 Ashes in Australia, news broke that Mark Waugh and Shane Warne had accepted money from an Indian bookmaker, apparently in exchange for pitch and weather information during Australia's tour of Sri Lanka in 1994. The Australian Cricket Board (ACB) fined them, but kept the whole thing quiet. Once the story got out, the Barmy Army was in no mood to let them off so easily.

(to the tune of 'My Old Man's a Dustman')

Mark Waugh is an Aussie
He wears a baggy cap
And when he saw the bookie's cash
He said 'I'm having that'
He shared it out with Warney
They went and had some beers
And when the ACB found out
They covered it up for years

WHAT THEY SAY
BARMY ARMY

'This is Wildean wit compared with the one-word chant of "Ingerlund" favoured by football supporters.'

— The *Financial Times*. No, really.

'I CAN'T READ'

Ricky Ponting's early years as an international cricketer were punctuated with a number of 'incidents' involving alcohol. During the 1998–99 ODI series with England and Sri Lanka, he was involved in a fight outside a pub in the Kings Cross district of Sydney, earning himself a three-match suspension and a black eye. Manna from heaven for the Barmy Army songwriters . . .

(to the tune of 'Polly Wolly Doodle')

I can't read and I can't write
I must be Australian
I can't read and I can't write
I must be Australian

I can't bowl and I can't bat
My name's Ricky Ponting
I can't drink and I can't fight
My name's Ricky Ponting

WHAT THEY SAY   BARMY ARMY

'I have said for a long time that the Barmy Army are the best sporting crowd in the world. I don't care what sport you are talking about, or what country – they are unbelievably good supporters. There is never anything untoward, it is always good light-hearted stuff, and when England have a sniff of winning the volume goes up tenfold. They add a lot to the whole experience of the Ashes.'

— Fair play to Ricky, he might have given us a fair bit of ammo, but he's never complained when we choose to use it.

'LANGER IS AN AUSSIE'

During the 2002–03 Ashes tour, the Barmy Army had picked up on Brett Lee's suspect bowling action. We took great delight in calling 'no-balls' regularly. Although this didn't seem to have much effect on Lee himself, it did on Justin Langer, who called us a disgrace before going on to say: 'These people stand behind a fence drinking beer, with most of them 50 kilos overweight, making ridiculous comments. It's easy for someone to say that from behind a fence.' This was not the smartest thing he had ever done. As well as greeting him with the theme song to the seven dwarves, in reference to his diminutive stature, and singing songs about ourselves being 50 kilos overweight while he was 50 centimetres underheight, we also regaled him with this ditty.

(to the tune of 'My Old Man's a Dustman')

Langer is an Aussie

He wears the gold and green

He is the biggest whinger

That we have ever seen

He wasn't very happy

When we called Brett Lee's no-ball

He's got a very big mouth

And he's only five feet tall

WHAT THEY SAY

'I am expecting to get both barrels from the Barmy Army, but like I keep saying to the Barmy Army, as loyal as they are to England, I'm as loyal to my team-mates. When you have two loyal groups, there's always going to be a bit of heat there, so we'll see what happens. If I don't make any runs I'll be grumpy and I won't like them, if I make runs I'll be happy. I've learned my lesson, don't worry.'

— Justin Langer preparing to front up to the Army again in 2006.

'Needless to say the Barmy Army were always all over me at games, but it was always fun.'

— Langer sees it slightly differently after retirement.

EXTRAS

To be fair to Langer he did mellow. One photo shows him signing the belly of one corpulent England fan and during the final Test of the 2006–07 series was happy to oblige when we called him to 'give us a wave' as he was batting in his last innings.

'RICKY PONTING'

There's absolutely no reason to refer to Ponting as a drag queen, and in terms of political correctness it's probably the wrong side of the line. But Ricky Ponting always left himself wide open to Barmy Army abuse and this is just plain funny.

(to the tune of 'My Old Man's a Dustman')

**Ponting is the captain
Of the Aussie cricket team
But once the match is over
He is a gay drag queen
Ponting's special friend
Is a man called Glenn McGrath
You'll see them holding hands
At the Sydney Mardi Gras**

WHAT THEY SAY

BARMY ARMY

'Isn't it great, when you consider the rivalry which used to exist between Glenn as a player and the Barmy Army as a support crew that we're now in a stage where they are totally supportive of everything we are trying to do.'

— McGrath Foundation CEO, Kylie Tink, recognises the work the Barmy Army does to raise money for his organisation.

'SHANE WARNE IS AN AUSSIE'

We're not really sure how Glenn McGrath got away without having a litany of songs written about him, while Warney was the butt of several, but boy did he give us a ton of ammunition.

(to the tune of 'My Old Man's a Dustman')

Shane Warne is an Aussie
He wears a baggy cap
He's got a Nike earring
He looks an Aussie prat
He's got his little flipper
He's got his box of tricks
But when he bowls to Freddie
He gets knocked for six

WHAT THEY SAY   BARMY ARMY

'The England supporters are also very good at dishing it out. They overstepped the mark a few times with songs about me, but I really enjoyed the part the Barmy Army played in games.'

— Shane Warne shows that there are no hard feelings. Well, not many anyway. The 'overstepping' was a reference to chanting 'where's your missus gone' after his divorce. But then it's not like he was an innocent party in that.

'SHANE WARNE IS AN AUSSIE' – PART TWO

Never far from controversy, Warney once got banned for taking a diuretic that he insisted his mum had given him. We weren't going to let that pass.

(to the tune of 'My Old Man's a Dustman')

Shane Warne is a druggie

He should be in rehab

He took his mummy's little pill

To try and lose the flab

He took it to lose weight

From all the pies and beer

But when the ICC found out

He got banned for a year

'SHANE WARNE'S VILLA'

He'd been done for colluding with a bookie and we'd written a song about it. He'd been done for diet pills and we'd written a song about it. Why not write a song about them both?

(to the tune of 'Amarillo')

Show me the way to Shane Warne's villa
He's got his diet pills under his pilla
A dodgy bookie from Manila
Nursey's on her mobile phone

(Repeat x3)

La-la lar la-la la-la lar
Fat Git
La-la lar la-la la-la lar
Take a bung
La-la lar la-la la-la lar
Warney where's your mobile phone?

'SIDDLE BY SIDDLE'

This song represents something of a watershed. Peter Siddle's a good cricketer, but we were used to writing songs trying to rile great cricketers. Previously, we'd never sung songs about the Australian cricket team not being very good because it would have been patent nonsense. We soon realised their decline offered up new lyrical possibilities.

(to the tune of 'Little by Little')

Siddle by Siddle

You bowl us everything we ever dreamed of

Siddle by Siddle

The wheels of your team are slowly falling off

Siddle by Siddle

You always bowl a ball that goes for four

And all the time

Ponting asks himself why are you really here?

Why are you really here?
Why are you really here?
Why are you really here?

WHAT THEY SAY   BARMY ARMY

'Siddle is a wanker.'

> If you think we were harsh on Siddle, the Swami
> Army – a bunch of Indian supporters jumping on our
> bandwagon – cut to the chase with this one. Nice.

'THE JOHNSON FAMILY'

When Mitchell Johnson's mum went on record slating his girl-friend (the word 'bitchy' was used), she not only upset her son and caused a bit of a rift in the family, but left him wide open to some Barmy banter. And the beginnings of a crowd–player relationship like no other.

(to the tune of 'The Addams Family')
His mother hates his missus
His missus hates his mother
They all hate one another
The Johnson family
De le la le de le la le de le la le

WHAT THEY SAY

BARMY ARMY

'I do feel I have unfinished business with England and their supporters.'

— Mitchell Johnson after one of his good days, taking six for 38 in Perth during the 2010–11 Ashes.

'HE BOWLS TO THE LEFT'

A slow burning mutual antagonism between Mitch and the Army had developed over one and a half Ashes series. It suddenly exploded into life with this simple yet stunningly effective chant that took hold almost overnight. The actions that quickly accompanied it, as everyone swayed from left to right as they sang, became one of the defining images of the 2010–11 Ashes series. You could almost feel sorry for Mitch.

He bowls to the left
He bowls to the right
That Mitchell Johnson
His bowling is shite

WHAT THEY SAY

'I thought the Mitchell Johnson song was hilarious. Every time he started an over at the MCG, a whole end was swaying, it was just fantastic. And it definitely got to him, there's no doubt about that.'

— Vaughan's *TMS* colleague Jonathan Agnew also revelled in the Johnson banter.

'Imagine if he gets out for a golden duck here.'

— One Barmy Army member is hopelessly optimistic as Mitch walks out to bat in Australia's second innings in Sydney. One ball later he was on his way back to the hutch, the Barmy Army went ballistic and Johnson's Ashes, and his misery, were over.

I WRITE
THE SONGS

NAME:
Giles Wellington aka Gilo

DAY JOB:
Independent financial adviser

What is the key to writing a successful song?

We usually adopt some simple rules. They must be supportive,
clean, ideally topical and then, most importantly, 'scan'. The first
three are rarely a problem, but deep into the night, as the beer
takes effect, what may 'scan' for one tipsy ear often doesn't for
another. The simple ones are often best – popular tunes that can
be picked up several rows or blocks away – combined with some
random supportive words obviously containing the player's name.

First song you came up with?

Plenty that didn't get further than my shower, including a remake
of Toto's 'Africa' during the 2004–05 series, which included the
lines 'We'll win the series in South Africa, then we'll win the

Ashes tooooo,' and turned out to be not as fanciful as I'd first thought. Maybe the Ally Cook song (page 98) was one of the first that took off, a collaboration completed in a Nagpur hotel just outside the ground after close of play on the fourth day of Cookie's debut Test.

Best song you've written?

Probably not for me to say. My favourite was relating to Ryan Sidebottom's hat-trick, written on St Patrick's Day to the tune of 'Sweet Molly Malone' (see page 102). But the ones that proved more popular were 'Take The Urn Home' (page 10) and Matty Prior's (page 114), which was written in the boot of a cab on a frightening five-hour journey from Delhi to Chandigarh in 2008. I was determined to write one for him after meeting him on the 2006 India tour where he'd been very keen on buying us drinks on more than one occasion. In my mind, he'd been harshly treated by the press and I wanted to pen something positive, with one line referring to a stray jellybean that had caused controversy the previous summer and another questioning the quality of the females in Hove (Matt's wife is from the area). I'm not sure I did a great job, but he gave it the thumbs up and it's still a favourite now.

Favourite song that's not yours?

Simon Jones' 'Men of Harlech' (page 73). I remember first singing it in a choir practice scenario in the Durban Hilton. Because of the many verses, we were all given song sheets.

Best Barmy Army singing memory?

I always enjoy it when we co-opt the players to join in. I have fond memories from the last night in New Zealand, when Harmy helped Monty lead the national anthem, but my favourite was after the Lord's Test during the 2009 Ashes series. We'd won around lunchtime, which is always dangerous as it leaves plenty of time to celebrate. About twelve of us caught up with the players in their hotel bar and after initial polite conversation, we burst into a few songs before we encouraged the players to lead us into a song each. First it was 'Swanny, Swanny give us a song, Swanny give us a song', and he immediately led us into a rendition of 'Jerusalem'. Then 'Cookie give us a song' went straight into 'We've got Tim Ambrose'. Finally, we built up the confidence for 'Straussy, Straussy give us a song, Straussy give us a song'. It went quiet. Strauss looked for inspiration from his lovely wife, Ruth, and then stood up and in full voice came out with 'Swanny is a wanker, Swanny is a wanker, lalalala, lalalala'. To be fair, Swanny joined in as it rang out around the hotel.

7 ENGLAND PLAYERS – THE MODERN ERA

Again it's a very rough type of dividing line, but by 'modern' we mean those who have come into the side since that 2005 Ashes win. It's now regarded as imperative that any player gets their own song on debut, so very few have come and gone without being serenaded to something, even if they played only one Test.

'ALLY, ALLY COOK'

Alastair Cook was playing for the ECB National Academy in the West Indies when he was called to India at late notice to replace Marcus Trescothick in the senior side. He didn't exactly get off the plane and go straight to the stadium, but it was as near as dammit. And he took to international cricket like the Barmy Army to Kingfisher lager, scoring a century in his first match. Time for some KC & the Sunshine Band.

(to the tune of 'Give It Up')

You flew out to India
When your country needed you
Century on debut, what a find
Na na na na na na na na na
Ally Ally Cook, Ally Cook, Ally Ally Cook
Na na na na na na na na na

WHAT THEY SAY

'When we went into the Aussie dressing room for a drink on Friday afternoon after our victory, even their players were singing Barmy Army songs.'

— Alastair Cook explains that it's not just the England players who think their songs are catchy.

EXTRAS

The Barmy Army songwriters had a tough challenge when two other players made their debuts in the same match as Cook. Their efforts for Cook and Panesar were worth the effort; unfortunately for Ian Blackwell he would play only one Test, which is a shame as his song's much better than Monty's ...

'MONTY PANESAR'

Monty Panesar was always going to be a Barmy Army legend. His appearance, his dodgy fielding, his ridiculously enthusiastic attitude and his passionate, child-like celebrations were immediately endearing. His song wasn't even really a song, it contained no words other than his name, but do you think he cares?

(to the tune of 'Papa's Got a Brand New Pigbag')

De de de de
Monty Panesar
De de de de
Monty Panesar
(Repeat ad infinitum)

> ## WHAT THEY SAY BARMY ARMY
>
> 'I enjoyed being a cult hero. I didn't expect it, but the warmth and love the fans gave me, even in the bad times, was wonderful. They never turned against me. Between overs, on the boundary edge, they'd say, "Chin up, son. Next over, you'll get him." The Barmy Army love me.'
>
> — Monty makes us go all a bit mushy inside.

'IAN BLACKWELL'

Ian Blackwell bowled only 114 deliveries in his one and only Test match, but he still managed to inspire a Donovan rewrite based on a press article where he revealed his love for, and need to cut down on, toasted sandwiches.

(to the tune of 'Mellow Yellow')

He eats ham and cheese toasties
Polishes them off for his tea
Left arm bowler for England
Smashes every delivery

They call him Ian Blackwell
That's right
They call him Ian Blackwell

EXTRAS

No extras, just 19 overs, two maidens, nought for 71. An entire Test career summed up in one fragment of a sentence.

'SIDEBOTTOM, SIDEBOTTOM'

Ryan Sidebottom's song was written during his first overseas Test in Kandy, Sri Lanka. The version you see below is the final edit that came as a result of his hat-trick during a Test in New Zealand. Prior to that the song ended with the words 'He bats at number eight, he likes to masturbate'. We knew something was slightly wrong about it, but at the same time it was so right so we continued to sing the original version on occasions.

(to the tune of 'Robin Hood')

Sidebottom, Sidebottom
Swings it through the air
Sidebottom, Sidebottom
With his curly hair

He bats at eight or nine
His hat-trick was sublime
Sidebottom, Sidebottom
Sidebottom

WHAT THEY SAY   BARMY ⚑ ARMY

'I suppose I like the rude version best. I think my mum likes
it, you know. It gets everyone laughing, and I don't mind.'

— If it's good enough for Ryan, surely it's
good enough for us – rude or not.

EXTRAS

Ryan can now be seen modelling Barmy Army merchandise at
www.barmyarmy.com.

'THREE IN A ROW'

Relevance is a word that comes up a lot when people talk about
what makes a good Barmy Army song. Few are more relevant
than this one. It contains the place, the situation, the event and
the details of that event. (If it's not obvious enough, the match
was played in Hamilton, England scored at two runs per over
in the entire game, Ryan Sidebottom got a hat-trick, two of
them were caught by opener Ally Cook.) And if that's not
enough, it's an Irish tune and was written on St Patrick's Day.

(to the tune of 'Sweet Molly Malone')

In Hamilton city

Where the batting was gritty

I first saw our Ryan get three in a row

He bowled left arm over

Got 'em caught by our opener

That's when our Ryan got three in a row

Three in a row

Three in a row

With Fleming, Sinclair and Jacob Oram

WHAT THEY SAY

'I caught the catch that won the second Test in front of the Barmy Army, which was a great feeling. They've been fantastic in their support, which puts two or three per cent on your performance, especially when they're shouting your name.'

— Sidebottom espouses his love of the Army.

'I think he's just bowled us to defeat.'

— Songwriter Giles Wellington's pessimistic statement immediately after the hat-trick. He was proved 100 per cent correct.

'WE'VE GOT TIM AMBROSE'

Wicket-keeper Tim Ambrose played only 11 Test matches, just four of them overseas. But this rather nonsensical ditty became hugely popular. Why we didn't immediately get on the phone

to Ambrosia and ask for some sponsorship as their products were hawked around New Zealand's cricket grounds is something we're probably still kicking ourselves for.

(to the tune of 'You Are My Sunshine')

We've got Tim Ambrose

Sounds like Ambrosia

They make good custard

Comes in a tin

They make Creamed Rice too

That's not important

Just as long as England win

WHAT THEY SAY

'I love my song.'

— Tim Ambrose keeping his appreciation succinct.

'I hope Timmy Ambrose gets a shout out because it is still the best Barmy Army song ever.'

— Graeme Swann wants to hear the song again, even if the man himself isn't playing any more.

'HE'S BIG, HE'S BAD'

When Stuart Broad broke into the team, we knew little about him other than the fact that he was tall and his dad had played for England. We now know quite a lot more, but have still to create anything more meaningful than this. On turning down an IPL contract to concentrate on playing for England, it did have a brief shelf life as: 'He's tall, bowls well, turned down the IPL', but if writing songs about Stuart Broad was a school subject then the Barmy Army teacher would no doubt say 'Must do better'.

(to the tune of 'The Quartermaster's Store')

He's big, he's bad
He's better than his dad
Stuart Broad, Stuart Broad

WHAT THEY SAY

'I can't wait to hear the Barmy Army's new songbook.'

— Stuart Broad obviously likes our work, but we're guessing there must be a bit of him hoping for something a little more sophisticated with his name in it.

'JUST A LITTLE BIT'

Kevin Pietersen had been in the England team for three years and had been its best player during that time. But we had never got round to singing any kind of song about him, despite his heroics. Many felt his ego was big enough without needing a Barmy Army massage, but by the New Zealand tour of 2008 we thought this was a bit churlish and set out to write a song about him. We ended up with several, but none better than the following, inspired by the fact that Mrs KP is Jessica Taylor, formerly of Liberty X, whose most famous song was 'Just a Little', as we're sure everyone recalls.

(to the tune of 'Just a Little')

KP
When you walk out to the crease,
You're sexy
You are England's number four
You've got a ton to score
So . . .

Hook! Just a little bit
Pull! Just a little bit
Drive! Just a little bit
Score just a little bit more
KP score a little bit more
Just a little bit more, just a little bit

EXTRAS

A day or two after this song was written, four Barmy Army foot soldiers somehow found themselves serenading the wives and girlfriends with a variety of songs. They called JV, the writer of this song, and he was surprised to find himself singing his new opus directly down the phone to Jessica.

'HI HO SUPER KP'

Meanwhile, we had been interrogating Matthew Hoggard to try to get some inspiration. Ever helpful, Hoggy said we should engineer references to KP's earrings and the fact that his middle name is Peter into the lyrics. And so we did just that with some Jeff Beck influence.

(to the tune of 'Hi-ho Silver Lining')

You're our spinner and fourth in, KP
That's where you bat
Showing your bling at fourth slip
With your big bold tatts

Blinding us with your earrings
From where we're sat
You cut and drive the new ball
With your Woodworm bat

And it's hi-ho Super KP

Everywhere we go now, Peter

You'll score a double century

Or maybe just a ton

You're Kevin Pietersen

WHAT THEY SAY   BARMY ⚔ ARMY

'His middle name's Peter?'

— Everyone reacts with disbelief when Hoggy
reveals what the middle P stands for.

'HIS NAME IS KEVIN PIETERSEN'

If one of the keys to writing a successful song is choosing a tune that everyone knows, then this is the exception that proves the rule. No one had heard of this Gogol Bordello 'classic' other than the writer and, when we finally downloaded it, his version wasn't particularly close to the original anyway.

(to the tune (loosely) of 'Start Wearing Purple')

He's got an average over fifty

He likes to score a massive ton

His ego's bigger than his batty

His name is Kevin Pietersen

WHAT THEY SAY

'My own little ditty underwent a slight change following Jessica's [Pietersen's wife] revelation that KP thought it was about him having a big bum. Originally it was "batting", but "batty" means bum in South Africa so "His ego's bigger than his batty" it is then. Thanks Jessica – priceless.'

— Writer Adrian Raffill explains a change in the lyrics inspired by a misinterpretation.

'GET KP'

During the 2010–11 Ashes series, KP inspired a new song about his batting after an imperious double century. Such is the fast-moving nature of cricket, though, that no sooner had it been penned than another verse was required . . .

(to the tune of 'Let It Be')

When we find ourselves in times of trouble
Andy Flower says to me
We need a batting hero, get KP
Get KP, get KP, get KP
Smashing fours and sixes, get KP

As he raised his bat unto the Army
Having scored his double century

England's batting hero, he's KP
He's KP, he's KP, he's KP, he's KP
Smashing fours and sixes, he's KP

At Adelaide, it was late on Monday
Michael Clarke he'd scored eighty
We need a bowling hero, get KP
Get KP, get KP, get KP, get KP
Taking Clarkey's wicket, that's KP

WHAT THEY SAY   BARMY ARMY

'We have the best supporters in the world. Period!!'

— KP says it all with Twitter.

'SWANNY SUPER OVER'

Graeme Swann made his England Test debut against India in Chennai in a series that had been hastily rearranged after the Mumbai terrorist attacks. Because of the change in schedule, the Barmy Army's travel plans went out the window and they rearranged flights to get to the newly assigned venues. When Swann bowled his first over, the first ball went straight to the boundary. His third accounted for Gautam Gambhir and his sixth was good enough to dismiss Rahul 'The Wall' Dravid.

Forearmed with the knowledge that Swann is a big Oasis fan, the Barmy Army got to work.

(to the tune of 'Champagne Supernova')

How many special people came
So many flights we had to change
Where were you when we were in Chennai?

Got hit for four with his first ball
Then took Gambhir and the Wall
Where were you when we were in Chennai?

Some day you will find him
Taking loads of wickets
In a Swanny super over in Chennai

Some day you will find him
Taking loads of wickets
In a Swanny super over, a Swanny super over

Because people believe
That we should never have come here at all
But you and I, will never die
And Graeme Swann is just one reason why, why, why,
    why . . .

WHAT THEY SAY   BARMY ARMY

'It's my favourite song because it was my first song and it was to Oasis, which was amazing because I love Oasis and it just makes me laugh, especially when everyone goes "Chennnnaiiii".'

— Graeme Swann never gets tired of the first Army song about him.

EXTRAS

A few variations of this song evolved, and the last verse has now been changed to 'Because we all believe/That he can take a wicket a ball'.

For all his professed love of the song, Swanny has never bothered to learn the lyrics, although he has been known to sing along with a bit of prompting.

'GRAEME SWANN IS BOWLING'

During a warm-up match for the 2009–10 tour of South Africa, Swann took three wickets in four balls. The last wicket he partly attributed to the fact that the batsman was still laughing at a quip made by Matt Prior: 'There are two things you should never do: cut a spinner and pat a burning dog.' A song lyric if ever we'd heard one.

(to the tune of 'My Old Man's a Dustman')

Oh Graeme Swann is bowling

He's going to get you out

Whenever it is turning

He'll always have a shout

And when he takes a wicket

He'll tweet it on his blog

So never cut a spinner or pat a burning dog!

WHAT THEY SAY

'I think that's already a given. We have the bugler, we can get someone to play the drums as there's always a lot of banging and then me. It can be like Mumford & Sons.'

— Swanny prepares to write an album with the Barmy Army.

'SWANN WILL TEAR YOU APART'

Short and simple. As Graeme Swann smashed 85 from 81 balls in the first Test against South Africa in 2009–10, this one came out of nowhere. Originally used only when he was batting, it's now ubiquitous whenever he is in the action.

(to the tune of 'Love Will Tear Us Apart')

Swann, Swann will tear you apart again

Swann, Swann will tear you apart again

WHAT THEY SAY

'What a brilliant night with the best travelling support in the world. Barmy Army I salute you.'

— Swanny tweets after celebrating the 2010–11 Ashes win.

'HE'S MATTY PRIOR'

Perhaps the greatest mangling of the English language in Barmy Army history uses the verb 'enquire' where it should be a noun, but who cares? The Johnny Cash classic 'Ring of Fire' had been one of Billy the Trumpet's favourites ever since the England boys had used it to gee themselves up before a victory against India in 2006. Prior. Fire. It didn't take a genius to link those together. Throw in some references to the jellybean incident against India in 2008, his lack of hair and big hitting and a song is born.

(to the tune of 'Ring of Fire')

He always takes the top-edge skier

He bats at Hove where his average gets higher

Four, six, four
He's Matty Prior, he's Matty Prior

He got caught in the jellybean enquire
He plays at Hove where the women are dire
Four, six, four
He's Matty Prior, he's Matty Prior

He's got no need for a Brylcreem supplier
He never uses the hotel hairdryer
Four, six, four
He's Matty Prior, he's Matty Prior

EXTRAS

The Barmy Army's PR guru Becky Fairlie-Clarke is from Hove.
She can be heard, along with her husband Allan, shouting 'He
comes from Hove where the women are on fire' over the rest of
the Barmy Army masses.

Prior is one of the Barmy Army's biggest fans and can often
be seen encouraging us to sing up and then dancing along
behind the stumps as we do.

'JONNY TROTTER'

Trott. Trotter. Not a particularly sophisticated link, but one that came immediately to mind when we sat at The Oval in 2009 watching him score a century on debut against the Australians. That, allied to the fact he was born in South Africa, led to the following. Hardly anyone remembers the lyrics, but Bill still plays the tune when Trott is involved.

(to the tune of 'Only Fools and Horses')

Stick your passport in your pocket
And your kitbag in the van
'Cos if you want the Ashes
And you don't mind Saffers
Then brother, he's your man

'Cos where he comes from is no mystery
But he's gonna lead us home to an Ashes victory
A song for him was driving us berserk
But then we thought that Jonny Trotter works

La-la-la-la-la la-la-la-la-la-la

WHAT THEY SAY

BARMY ARMY

'They sing a couple of songs about me. One is set to the tune of "Only Fools and Horses", I guess it is the Trott and Trotter link, and I quite like listening to the rhythm of it. I take it as a compliment.'

— Only Jonny Trott(er) would talk about the rhythm of the song.

ENGLAND'S NUMBER THREE

Using the same inspiration as his first song, this is now the *de rigueur* Barmy Army anthem for 'England's number three'.

(to the tune of 'When Johnny Goes Marching Home')

He left the Cape to wear three lions

Trotty, Trotty

He scored a ton to win the urn

Trotty, Trotty

He hits the ball, it goes for four

He plays the shots we all adore

Jonny Trott is England's number three

Na na na na

WHAT THEY SAY   BARMY  ARMY

'I enjoy every minute when they are singing. I know the team enjoy it and it lifts us. I wish we could express our appreciation in a better manner.'

— Here's a hint, Jonny – buy us beer.

'YOU CAN'T HURRY TROTT'

When Trott's original songs were written, we didn't know much about him, but three years later and his unhurried, meticulous approach to batting endeared him to us in a way that would have infuriated us if he wasn't wearing the three lions.

(to the tune of 'You Can't Hurry Love')

You can't hurry Trott,
No, you just have to wait
(She said) Runs don't come easy
It's a game of 'Yes, no, wait'

You can't hurry Trott
No, you just have to wait
Just trust in his batting
No matter how long it takes
Now wait!

118

EXTRAS

Trott missed out on the Barmy Army party after the 2010–11 Ashes because he was too busy lining up his underpants. (This may not be true. OK, it's definitely not true, but we wouldn't be surprised if he has the days of the week written on his underwear.)

'DING DONG BELLY IS OUR KING'

It might seem heretical to compare Ian Bell to Don Bradman, but seeing as the great man scored 6,996 runs in his career, Bell may well overtake him and then he really will 'score more runs than Bradman'. So there.

(to the tune of 'Ding Dong Merrily On High')

Ding dong Belly is our King
He's England shortest batsman
Ding dong Belly is our King
He'll score more runs than Bradman
La la la la la la la la la la

There was a song about Ian Bell that was sung to the tune of Jingle Bells, but for some reason (and not just because it was a Christmas song) it never really took off. Which was pretty embarrassing when we sang to the players' wives and his lovely other half, Chantal, asked us what our song for him was. Cue embarrassing silence.

'THE NAAN SONG'

If Tim Bresnan hadn't made his overseas debut in Bangladesh, who knows what we would have come up with? Naan bread is up there with Ambrosia in terms of tenuous connections, but we love it all the more for that.

(to the tune of 'Those Were The Days')

We've had a garlic naan

We've had a butter naan

We've had a plain, we've had a keema too

But our favourite naan, is Tim Bresnan

All because he hates the convicts too

WHAT THEY SAY   BARMY ARMY

'How to make 75,000 empty seats vibrate. Let the Barmy Army sing. Unbelievable support from the best supporters in the world.'

— Bresnan loves a beer with the Army and a tweet about them.

'STEVEN FINN'

When Steven Finn came into the England side, it didn't take long for the Barmy Army's lyricists to spot the opportunity for adapting the Manfred Mann song 'The Mighty Quinn' to incorporate his name in the words. Indeed, the link was such a natural one that not everyone noticed it straight away.

(to the tune of 'The Mighty Quinn')

He swings it out

Comes steaming in

He's gonna knock 'em over

He's Steven Finn

WHAT THEY SAY

'We should write a song about Steve Finn to the tune of "The Mighty Quinn".'

— Doug Mulholland, writer of the Jesse Ryder classics on pages 135–7. Nothing unusual about his comment, except for the fact that he'd been singing this one for several days already.

'CHRISSY TREMLETT'

Whenever a Test match is played in the run-up to Christmas, it opens up some obvious yuletide opportunities. And so when

Tremlett came into the side just before Christmas 2010 we came up with this. Not sure what we do during the rest of the year.

(to the tune of 'Merry Christmas Everybody')

So here he is, Chrissy Tremlett
Bowling fast for England
He's got a future now
The convicts on the run

EXTRAS

Another yuletide favourite is 'Twelve Days of Christmas' that is rewritten every series, but always ends with 'Four more runs, three proud lions, two cheating umpires and a win at the SCG' where 'the SCG' is whatever ground we happen to be in.

'JIMMY ANDERSON'

On the one hand there are no words to be learned in order to sing Jimmy's 'song', so it's usually one of the loudest. On the other hand he's upset that he hasn't got something a bit more inventive.

Oohh Jimmy Jimmy
Jimmy Jimmy Jimmy
Jimmy Anderson

WHAT THEY SAY   BARMY ARMY

'Please write me a better song.'

— Jimmy makes his opinion clear.

'JAMES, YOU'RE TOO GOOD TO BE TRUE'

This song has only been sung about four times in Sri Lanka, but for Jimmy's sake we've added it here so people can learn it and sing it in future.

(to the tune of 'Can't Take My Eyes Off You')

James, you're too good to be true
You bowl so fast and so true
Batting line-ups you will run through
I can't take my eyes off of you

James when you make it swing
The Barmy Army will sing
You're our nightwatchman too
The Burnley Lara are you

Der de, der de, der de de de etc

Oh Jimmy Anderson
When you bowl right arm fast

Oh Jimmy Anderson

The batsmen never last

Oh Jimmy Anderson

Take a wicket for me

Oh Jimmy Anderson

When you get the ball

Oh Jimmy Anderson

The wickets start to fall

Oh take a wicket Jimmy

Take a wicket

WHAT THEY SAY   BARMY ARMY

'Please get everyone singing that one.'

— Jimmy expresses approval.

I WRITE THE SONGS

NAME:
Paul Winslow aka Winslow

DAY JOB:
Magazine editor, website editor, journalist, author

What is the key to writing a successful song?

It has to be easy for people to pick up. There's a reason so many songs use the same basic tunes, and it's because they are so easily adapted and easily remembered. I usually get told off for trying to write songs that are too complicated. For the more in-depth ones to work, you really need a small group of people to learn it first and then hope it gradually takes off. That's easier to do on a small tour, when others are less likely to sing over a group trying to get a song off the ground. When you're on a small tour with a lot of the hardcore, it's much easier to get something new going than in Australia, where people just sing over you and are not so bothered about starting something new because they may be busy enjoying the classics for the first time.

First song you came up with?

The Tim Ambrose one (see page 103) in New Zealand, 2008. Ironically, I didn't think it was anything special when I wrote it – I mean it was basically a song about tinned dessert products. A week later everyone was singing it, including the players, so obviously it struck a chord somewhere. I've written better ones that have been dismissed out of hand by the songwriters' union, but somehow that one got through. It did help when he scored a century in the Test after it was first aired.

Best song you've written?

It has to be 'Swanny Super Over' (page 110). I knew he was an Oasis fan, as he was always mentioning them in his *All Out Cricket* column, so I was insistent that we use a tune from the Gallaghers. It was actually Heather Storry who started off with the idea of Swanny Supernova, someone else made it Swanny Super Over and the rest came from there. I've been lucky enough to meet him a few times and had the chance to sing it with him. Knowing how much he loves it makes it pretty special.

Favourite song that's not yours?

I absolutely love the Shaun Pollock song (page 131). I know it's a rework of the original Allan Donald song, so maybe I should include them both, but I love the fact they use a song that's a bit different, that they are relevant, piss-taking without being cruel and incredibly catchy. I really enjoy songs that are relevant to a person's background or events on the field, which is why the Simon Jones 'Men of Harlech' and KP's 'Just a Little' are also among my favourites.

Best Barmy Army singing memory?

Singing Swanny's song on a bar with him after the win in Melbourne; ten people singing in the sea at 7 a.m. in Unawatuna after the 2012 Galle Test; singing the Dan Vettori song in joke glasses; thirty people entertaining themselves for five days of a dull Test match in Mohali, 2008. That's more than one moment and there are many others I've not mentioned.

8 OPPOSITION PLAYERS – REST OF THE WORLD

Without the intense rivalry that Australia and England share, writing about opposing players from other sides has never been so much of a preoccupation. But when someone does something that is deserving of a song, there's no point leaving it unwritten.

'ALLAN DONALD'

During the World Cup semi-final in 1999, South Africa needed just one more run for victory. Lance Klusener mishit the ball, but decided to risk the run. Unfortunately Allan Donald was busy a) ensuring he wasn't run out at the non-striker's end and b) dropping his bat. By the time he realised Klusener had run, they were both at the same end. He was run out and Australia went through by virtue of their win over South Africa in a Super 6 game. It had nothing to do with us, but inspired one of the all-time great songs to The Crystals classic.

(to the tune of 'Da Do Ron Ron')

My name is Allan Donald and I should have run

Run, run Alan, run, run, run

Zulu called a single but I stood still

Run, run Alan, run, run, run

Oh I had a panic attack

Oh and I dropped my bat

Oh I should have run

Run, run Alan, run, run, run

EXTRAS

If it wasn't bad enough having the Barmy Army continually sing this at you, it's reported that Donald's team-mates used to sing it to him in the nets. One of those team-mates was Shaun Pollock, but what goes around, comes around . . .

'SHAUN POLLOCK'

You really couldn't have written it, but it did happen so we did write it. During the following World Cup, held in South Africa in 2003, the home side were playing Sri Lanka in a rain-affected match that meant the Duckworth-Lewis method had come into play. Mark Boucher was batting, but having hit a six from the penultimate ball he got the nod from Pollock that this would be enough to see South Africa through and played out a dot ball to finish the innings. But Pollock had made a mistake and they actually needed one more run. South Africa lost the game and were knocked out of the World Cup. Making up a song after this was like shooting fish in a barrel . . .

(to the tune of 'Da Do Ron Ron')

My name is Shaun Pollock and I cannot count
One more run run, one more run
I miscalculated and we got knocked out
One more run run, one more run
Oh I had a panic attack
Oh and I got the sack
Oh we needed one more run
One more run run, one more run

'MURALI'S SONG'

The Australians hate Murali and some of them think he chucked his way to 800 wickets. We couldn't bring ourselves to hate him as he seemed such a nice bloke, and anyone who gets up the Australians' nose has very redeeming features. But at the same time, we couldn't let the situation pass without writing a song about it.

(to the tune of 'Row, Row, Row Your Boat')

Throw, throw, throw the ball
Gently though the air
Murali, Murali, Murali, Murali
Where is Darrell Hair?
Throw, throw, throw the ball
Gently down the seam
Murali, Murali, Murali, Murali
Chucks it like a dream

WHAT THEY SAY

'Maybe he doesn't quite understand what we are getting at, or maybe he's just a good sport. I think he doesn't mind personally.'

—In the absence of any comment from Murali, Paul Burnham's opinion is all we have to go on.

'SHAHID AFRIDI'S SONG'

When England toured Pakistan in 2005, there was a break in play during the second Test when a gas canister exploded. While everyone else's attention was directed towards what was happening with the disturbance, Shahid Afridi decided to start spinning around on the pitch to scuff it up. Even without people seeing it on TV, umpire Darrell Hair noticed, as did Marcus Trescothick. A three-match ban was on its way – as was Barmy Army immortality.

(to the tune of 'Let's Twist Again')

Let's twist again
Like Shahid Afridi
Let's twist again
Like we did last Test
Do you remember when
You got caught for cheating?

Let's twist again
Twisting time is here

Because he was banned, we never got to sing it to him on that tour, although it did get a very brief outing at a home Test match when Pakistan were in England.

'DAN VETTORI'

Erm, Daniel Vettori wears glasses. Harry Potter wears glasses. Sophisticated it ain't. Amusing it is.

(to the tune of 'Oh, My Darling Clementine')
Dan Vettori
Dan Vettori
Harry Potter in disguise
We are going to
Steal your glasses
And poke you in the eyes

EXTRAS

This song is even funnier when one of the Barmy Army visits a joke shop at lunchtime and comes back with a bag full of fake Harry Potter glasses for everyone to wear while singing it.

'JESSE RYDER'S SLOOP JOHN B'

Jesse Ryder was expected to be part of the New Zealand Test team for the 2008 tour. But when he badly cut his hand trying to break into a toilet in Christchurch, he found himself out of the Test team and in Christchurch Hospital. It inspired not one, but two Barmy Army classics.

(to the tune of 'Sloop John B')

We came over from old Blighty
The Barmy Army and me
Around New Zealand's towns we did roam
Drinking all night
A grand for the flight
Well I feel a bit drunk now
I should have gone home

(Chorus)
So hoist up the John B sail
See how the mainsail sails
Call for the captain ashore
Let me go home
I wanna go home, I should have gone home
Well I feel a bit drunk now
I should have gone home

Jesse Ryder's an evil man
He gets drunk whenever he can
He doesn't give a toss
About Vettori and the boys

Jesse Ryder's a sod
He thinks he's a god
When he felt so drunk then
He should have gone home

(Repeat Chorus)

Now Jesse Ryder he got drunk
He smashed a window to have a dump
The constable had to come and take him away
Sheriff John Stone
Why don't you leave Jesse alone
When he felt so drunk then
He should have gone home

(Repeat Chorus)

'WHY, WHY, WHY, JESSE RYDER?'

(to the tune of 'Delilah')

I saw the rage in his eye as he looked for a toilet

I saw the glass on his hand as he smashed down the
door

I stood there laughing

He saw the blood on his sleeve and we laughed no more

(Chorus)

Why, why, why, Jesse Ryder?

Why, why, why, Jesse Ryder?

Long before the selectors say no more

Forgive me Vettori, I won't be a git any more

As Jesse woke up paralytic, in Christchurch Hospital

The doctor came in to offer Jesse a hand

But Jesse was still mortalled he said

(Spoken) Well I've had just about enough of you, so you
can go and . . .

(Repeat Chorus)

WHAT THEY SAY   BARMY ARMY

'I'd just like to thank the Barmy Army for not writing a song about me.'

New Zealand's captain Stephen Fleming, during his retirement speech after the 2008 series that spawned the Jesse Ryder songs.

EXTRAS

These are possibly the only songs ever written by the Barmy Army that haven't really been sung to the subject. As Ryder didn't play in that series, he escaped being at the sharp end. Does he realise what is coming his way when England tour there in 2013?

'YOU'VE GOT CHRIS MARTIN'

Chris Martin made his Test debut in 2000, the same year Coldplay released their 8.5-million-selling album *Parachutes*. One of these events led to an inoffensive and seemingly unremarkable fast bowler taking 226 Test wickets. The other led to over a decade of appalling bilge* being foisted on the world by a man who married Gwyneth Paltrow before calling his children Apple and Moses.

(to the tune of 'You Are My Sunshine')

You've got Chris Martin

He's not in Coldplay

He's not had Gwyneth

He cannot sing

He's got no albums

Or record contracts

But he's just as boring

EXTRAS

*I do realise the irony of dissing the songwriting skills of one of the most popular artists of his generation when we just nick popular tunes and twist them a bit. And the opinion on the subject of Chris Martin is clearly the author's and not that of the Barmy Army as a whole. But the fact is I'd rather go and see the fast bowler in concert.

What is the key to writing a successful song?

It depends on your definition of successful: if the criteria are simply for it to get picked up and sung repeatedly on tour then it just needs to be catchy, easily remembered and to a well-known tune. To elevate that to a 'classic' it also needs a witty reference to an incident on tour or something a player has said or done, preferably to a tune not used before.

First song you came up with?

'He's big, he's bad, he's better than his dad, Stuart Broad'. In Colombo, 2007 [Broad's Test debut] Billy the Trumpet turned to nobody in particular and said 'Quick, we need a song for Broad,' as he walked out to bat in the first innings. I blurted out the first thing that came into my head, which got the response 'he's *bad*?' but we went with it anyway. Sorry, Broady – my fault.

Best song you've written?

'Another Test Match in Galle'. That was also on the 2007 Sri Lanka tour at the third Test. This time, I had the opening two lines and the obvious chorus in my head at the ground, but couldn't think of how to get from one to the other. That night on the beach at Unawatuna I got Winslow (page 125) and Gilo (page 94) involved. Gilo immediately agreed it 'had legs', which is always a good response, and the rest was a collaborative effort. Many songs are. We can be in some of the best bars, the best restaurants, with the best views in the some of the best locations around the world and you'll find us hunched around a table scribbling on fag packets or napkins. It's very, very sad.

NB – We're glad Raff mentioned the Galle song, as it didn't fit neatly in a category, but here it is:

'ANOTHER TEST MATCH IN GALLE'

(to the tune of 'Another Brick in the Wall')

We don't need no seats to sit on

We don't need no stands at all

No more dodgy catches off the outfield

Harmy's going to bowl them all

Hey Umpire! Give us one good call
All in all it's just a-nother Test match in Galle

Favourite song that's not yours?

Swanny's 'Never cut a spinner' song (page 112). There are lots of songs to the tune of 'My Old Man's a Dustman', but this is an absolute classic. And 'Why, Why, Why, Jesse Ryder' (page 137) mostly because I was sat next to Doug Mulholland in the bar in Hamilton that he wrote it in and snorted beer out of my nose when I saw his opening line scrawled on a napkin.

Best Barmy Army singing memory?

A pub in Taylor Square, Sydney, after winning the 2003 Test. It was relatively empty when we arrived shortly after close of play, just a few locals and regulars, but it soon filled up to the point where you simply couldn't fit another person in there. Then someone started up 'We're the right side, we're the right side, we're the right side over here'. It's not normally one I much enjoy but the competition between right side, left side and middle to sing ever louder became hysterical. The visible, fervent effort on people's faces to belt it out was hilarious – I was hurting with laughter by the end. And serenading the players' wives pitchside in Napier in 2008 was pretty memorable.

9 THE SINGLES

In 1999 the World Cup came to England and the Barmy Army teamed up with Telstar Records, who had produced the hit single 'Vindaloo' for the 1998 football World Cup, to produce a single supporting the home team. There was a slight hiccup when the single was released a tad late, just as England were knocked out of the Super 6 stage of the tournament. 'Come On England' still managed to get to 46 in the charts and is memorable for a video that included Ian Botham, Dickie Bird, Ronnie Irani, Robin Smith and, erm, Chris Tarrant. The really surreal bit comes when Faye from Steps bowls to Hussein. And yes, we have spelled the surname correctly – it wasn't Nasser, but Saddam. Check it out on YouTube if you don't believe us. As for the song itself, it was a combination of commentary clips and a pretty unimaginative chorus that makes it about the worst composition in this book.

'COME ON ENGLAND'

Commentator: Well hello and welcome and a lovely day
here
Two hundred and eighty-eight to win and a lovely
partnership between Stewart and ...

(Chorus)
Barmy Army, shout it out
Barmy Army, shout it out
Come on England, shout it out
Come on England, shout it out
Barmy Army, shout it out
Come on England, shout it out

Commentator: The bowler's up to the wicket, he bowls ...
And Stewart has given that an almighty thump
It's going to be a six, it's going to be a six
And the crowd has gone absolutely wild

(Repeat Chorus)

Commentator: In comes Darren Gough, bowls, and he's
out
Yes, he's bottom edged onto the stumps.
He's out, yes, and the crowd goes absolutely wild here

(Repeat Chorus)

Commentator: Well the Barmy Army are enjoying
    themselves out there
How do you view them, David?
David Lloyd: Well they're a nice set of lads really
They love their cricket and they bring a wonderful
    atmosphere to the place

(Repeat Chorus to fade)

'HEY HEY RICKY'

During the build-up to the Ashes in 2009, the Barmy Army's thoughts again turned to releasing some kind of cricket record in support of the England team. We teamed up with Matt Jagger (no relation) to record 'Hey Hey Ricky'. Every good song (and, indeed, every bad one as well) needs a video, so a bunch of Barmy stalwarts convened at Stanmore cricket ground in North London to take part, helped out by a smattering of Marston's Maidens, *Sun* promo girls and various other interested parties. The video saw our 'Ricky' being harassed and chased around by the Barmy Army and the unleashing of the Ricky Roo – a dancefloor craze that swept the nation. OK, that last bit is a lie; it was occasionally seen at cricket grounds around the land as we attempted to promote it. It didn't really take off. Neither, sadly, did the record.

The *Sun* newspaper had promised to back the song, and with the power of the UK's biggest tabloid behind us, we felt there was a chance we could really do some damage. Unfortunately, another singer-songwriter by the name of Michael Jackson died on the day we released the single and for some reason the *Sun* decided to fill lots of pages about this Jackson bloke rather than getting behind our single. While it did get a few radio plays, it never made any impression on the charts.

(Chorus)
Hey Hey Ricky, what you gonna do?
Hey Hey Ricky, get on your kangaroo
We're taking back the Ashes, they don't belong to you
'Cos we're the Barmy Army, we're England through
    and through

You tried to find a bowler but it ended up in tears
You once had Warne and McGrath, now it's just that
    Brett Lee 'Spears'
You'll try to get a century, but we know how you bat
So go on back Down Under or we'll bring out Gary Pratt

(Repeat Chorus)

Symonds has gone fishing, Gilchrist is long gone
You have got no spinners, we've got Panesar and Swann

You'll always be a whinger, when will you ever learn
You'll never get your hands on our little Ashes urn

(Repeat Chorus)

You cook shrimps on the barbie, drink beer that's really
        weak
Your country isn't quite as old as some of our antiques
You didn't like our Bodyline, wish Beefy had been yours
Now we've got Freddie and KP to hit sixes and fours

(Repeat Chorus)

10 RANDOM SONGS ABOUT SHEDS, SALMON, SAUSAGES AND STANFORD

There are some songs that defy categorisation. The random songs that start this chapter off are nothing to do with cricket, indeed they're not much to do with anything and they are not our songs, but we sing them anyway. And then there are the results of a little challenge we set ourselves to write songs about Allen Stanford during his involvement with the Twenty20 for $20 million debacle where he financed a one-off game at his personal cricket ground with its sub-standard lighting. Apparently this gave him licence to flirt with the players' wives. Whatever happened to him?

'MY GARDEN SHED'

It's a favourite of football and rugby fans around the world, sung in reference to going to away grounds that are considered to be, shall we say, less than palatial. Not that we save it just for smaller grounds – we'd probably give it a crack in Eden Gardens for a bit of irony.

My garden shed
Is bigger than this
My garden shed is bigger than this
It's got a door and a window
My garden shed is bigger than this

'EVER HAD A TIN OF SALMON'

This is another football favourite, with lyrics as random as it really gets. There's no reference to cricket, but then there's no reference to football either. If you know where it originated, then you know more than we do.

Ever had a tin, ever had a tin
Ever had a tin of salmon
Ever had a tin of salmon spread
Here comes your mom with a loaf of bread

Oh salmon, oh salmon
Get it in a big tin, get it in a small tin
Get it from Tesco
All right

'I'D RATHER BE A SAUSAGE'

Did we say the last song was as random as it gets? Our mistake. Whether you actually would prefer to be a sausage than an egg is incidental. It's a classic to bring out when the opposition fans think you can't get any weirder.

I'd rather be a sausage than an egg
I'd rather be a sausage than an egg
I'd rather be a sausage
I'd rather be a sausage than an egg

Going szzz szzz szzz in a pan
Going szzz szzz szzz in a pan
Going szzz szzz szzz
Szzz szzz szzz
Szzz szzz szzz in a pan

'DREADLOCK HOLIDAY'

We never really had much chance to sing the Stanford songs as there was no Test series on at the time. But in all honesty we'd have been amazed if this took off because even the person who wrote it can never remember the words. But the song was quite apt considering his Caribbean background so we put it in here.

(To the tune of 'Dreadlock Holiday')

I was walkin' down the street
Concentratin' on struttin' right
Heard a loud voice beside of me
And I looked round in a state of fright
I saw a Texan, quite mad
A billionaire, oh brother
He looked me up and down a bit
We turned to each other

I say
I don't like Twenty20 oh no
I love it
I don't like Twenty20 no no
I love it
When you walk thru my ground
You got to show some respect

When you walk thru my ground
I ain't chatted to your wife yet

He asked me if I'd like to play a game
For twenty million dollar
I said you've got to be jokin' man
Can I bring along the others?
He said I got my own ground
It's just near where the aircraft lands
But when you agree, you'll soon see
You'd better understand that you're alone
A long way from home

And I say
I don't like reggae no no
I love it
I don't like reggae oh no
I love it
Don't you cramp Stanford's style
Don't you queer on his pitch
He's just one of those nerds
Who doesn't like real cricket yet

I hurried back to the dressing room
But the players were all over
They said we don't really want to stay

This thing is nonsense, moreover

Just because he's got his own ground

Test cricket is the best

And if he tries it he'll like it

No more of this Dreadlock Holiday

And I say

Don't like Antigua oh no

I love her

Don't like Antigua oh no

I love her oh yea

Don't you flirt with our birds

You got to show some respect

Just shut up with your words

Because we might not come back yet

I don't like Twenty20

I love it (Dreadlock Holiday)

I don't like reggae

I love it (Dreadlock Holiday)

Don't like Antigua

I love her (Dreadlock Holiday)

'HEY BIG SPENDER'

It's another example of a song where the original tune couldn't be more apt for the subject matter. In truth, any money-related song was always going to work when it came to such a ridiculous outlay of cash, although we still feel slightly bilious at the thought of a Texan swelling . . .

(to the tune of 'Big Spender')

The minute you flew into Lord's
I could see you were a man with a mission
A real big spender
'Tache bristling, not refined
The wags are beginning to see what's going on in your
     mind
So let me get right to the point
We don't want your sort, it's still our game you see?
Hey big spender
Spend . . . your dosh on baseball, not with me

The minute she sat on his lap
I could see a certain Texan swelling
Around midwicket
All the players, got the hump
She was only supposed to sit on his knee, not his
     middle stump.

So then he got right to the point:

'All this money, it's for just one thing, that's me!'

Hey big spender

Hey big spender

Hey big spender

Spend . . . your dosh on baseball, not with me

'MONEY MONEY MONEY

There's no shortage of money-related songs to choose from, so this was a pretty obvious place to start. It helped that the writer had a Swedish girlfriend at the time and was anxious to inject some Abba songs into the repertoire.

(to the tune of 'Money Money Money')

I bat all night, I bowl all day, to pay the bills I have to
     pay

Ain't it sad

And then Stanford came along he said

That's too bad

In my dreams I have a plan

It will make you a wealthy man

You won't have to work at all, just turn up and smack
     the ball

Money, money, money

Must be funny

In a Stanford world

Money, money, money

Always sunny

In a Stanford world

Aha-ahaaa

All the things I could do

If I had a little money

In a Stanford world

A man with so much cash, but still he's got a dodgy
    'tache

Ain't it sad

But his wicket's really slow and his floodlights are too
    low

That's too bad

And please don't flirt with our players' wives

'Cos you don't appreciate their cover drives

They win a fortune in your game, but compared to Tests
    it's really lame

11 CHRISTMAS CAROLS

We've often rejigged a variety of Christmas carols – an obvious route to take when in South Africa and Australia, as those tours encompass the yuletide period. In Mohali in 2008, we did an entire carol service replacing every word of every song with 'Owais Shah', but then we were a bit bored at that point. We've also been known to have 'real' carol services in Lord's ... in July. But during the 2010–11 Australia series one man wrote an entire service and yet he'd not been near a cricket ground. Mike O'Sullivan is the Barmy Army Finance Manager and spends most tours manning the phones at home. He put this lot together and sent them over, and little did he know the effect it would have. As the Barmy Army celebrated Christmas dinner at the Crown Entertainment Complex, they found themselves in the next room to the Australia cricket team. We can only guess that someone got in trouble for that, but there was no better opportunity to break out the carols in their honour.

'RICKY THE RED-FACED CAPTAIN

If it wasn't bad enough for Ricky that he was getting vilified because his team wasn't very good, in this song his batting is placed in the same bracket as a man who averaged 3.5 in the series. To be fair Ricky averaged only 16.14 in the 2010-11 Ashes so why not?

(to the tune of 'Rudolph the Red-Nosed Reindeer')

Ricky the red-faced captain
Leads a side in trouble and strife
Both he and Ryan Harris
Couldn't score to save their life

Strauss and his England teammates
Cooky, Bell and Kevin P
Showed how the Aussies are now
The worst team in their history

'HARK THE BARMY ARMY SING'

It would have been interesting to hear the Barmy Army give this one a crack in the grounds – we're not renowned for sounding like a choir, which is what this requires.

(to the tune of 'Hark the Herald Angels Sing')
Hark, the Barmy Army sing
Cheering England is our thing
Piece of pie and jug of beer
We're all full of Christmas cheer

We will raise our voices high
Ashes victory is nigh
Bumble's saying 'Start the car!'
We are the better team by far
Beaten in their own backyard
Aussies take that oh so hard
Hark, the Barmy Army sing
We'll have the urn, England is King!

'WE THREE SPINS'

Not content with saying we had a better team overall, this song points out that we've got better components as well.

(to the tune of 'We Three Kings')
We three spins of England are
Swann, KP and Panesar
Though Hauritz won't let her
His gran would do better
Warne was your spinning star

(Chorus)

Ohh, team of wonder

Team of might

Thrash the Aussies out of sight

Bowl 'em, catch 'em

Stump 'em, whack 'em

Till they wave a flag of white

We three bats of England are

Better than the Aussies by far

Scoring freely

Really easy

Your bowlers are under par

(Repeat Chorus)

We three quicks from far away

Aussie batsmen are our prey

Easy wickets

Won't be long till it's

All out by close of play

(Repeat Chorus)

Barmy Army soldiers are here

Chicken leg and weak Aussie beer

Jim and Billy

Acting silly

Give them some Christmas cheer

(Repeat Chorus)

'SILENT FANS'

No song collection would be complete without some friendly banter pointing out the rather quiet and unreliable nature of Australian cricket supporters.

(to the tune of 'Silent Night')

Silent fans

That's what you are

Nothing to sing

View from afar

Only turn up when your side's on top

Bet you wish that the slaughter would stop

When are you going to get better?

Or is spelling a challenge too far?

'BARMY ARMY IS ALL HERE'

By Christmas Day, the score was actually one-one so this wasn't perhaps the best song to be singing at the time, but little details like that never really worry us too much.

(to the tune of 'Good King Wenceslas')

The Barmy Army is all here
We wish you Merry Christmas
You may not like the songs we sing
But when we've gone you'll miss us
We're thrashing you by one to nil [to be amended as
     series result changes]
KP, Cook and Bell
When you come to England next
We'll thrash you there as weeeeeeeeeell

'O COME ON YOU ENGLAND'

There wasn't a great deal of Christmas spirit towards the Aussies in any of these songs, but this one begins in particularly Scrooge-like manner.

(to the tune of 'O Come All Ye Faithful')

O come on you England
Make Australia suffer

Grind down their will to live, and don't let go
Outscore their batsmen
Make their wickets tumble

(Chorus)
O come let us support them
O come let us support them
O come let us support them
E-ENG(er)LAND!

O come Barmy Army
Sing in exultation
Sing your support of England's
Great cricket team
Come and behold them
Whipping the Australians

(Repeat Chorus)

'ANDY FLOWER IS A MAESTRO'

This is something of a rarity. For some reason, we don't usually come up with songs about our coaches, which is something we should really rectify.

(to the tune of 'Deck the Halls')

Andy Flower is a maestro

Guides an England team, with little fuss

Aussies getting soundly beaten

Even Pakistan have bet on us

Not that we should get complacent

Couple of Test matches still to play

But can we see the Aussies winning?

That'll take forever and a day

'WE WISH YOU A BARMY TEST MATCH'

Another dose of wishing ill on our Aussie cousins that would have them striking us off their Christmas card list for the next year. Always assuming that we were ever likely to get on there in the first place.

(to the tune of 'We Wish You a Merry Christmas')

We wish you a Barmy Test match

We wish you a Barmy Test match

We wish you a Barmy Test match

You've had a bad year

(Chorus)

Glad tidings we bring

Cos you just can't win

We wish you a Barmy Test match
And another crap year

And you ain't got a chance of winning
You ain't got a chance of winning
You ain't got a chance of winning
You're not even near

(Repeat Chorus)

And we won't go without the Ashes
We won't go without the Ashes
We won't go without the Ashes
The urn's on its way here

(Repeat Chorus)

'ONCE IN ANDREW STRAUSS'S TEAM TALK'

Michael Clarke traditionally gets more abuse from the Aussie fans than he does from the English ones, but it was inevitable that he would get a mention eventually.

(to the tune of 'Once in Royal David's City')
Once in Andrew Strauss's team talk
Someone made a rude remark

'That's not what we call the Aussies!'
Was the captain's angry bark
'If you want to aggravate them
Should you want to leave your mark
Call them stupid Pommie convicts
That'll keep it simple, just like Clarke'

'AWAY IN AUSTRALIA'

Last but not least, a gentle and simple ditty that mentions hangovers and is quiet enough to not pierce the headache first thing in the morning.

(to the tune of 'Away in a Manger')
Away in Australia
No time for their beds
The Army were singing
And clearing their heads
We've won at the cricket
We've won in the bar
The only thing left is
Bidding Ricky 'au revoir'

WHAT THEY SAY

'My personal favourite of those that have been sung would probably be either "Ricky the Red-Faced Captain" or "Andy Flower is a Maestro". I'm the sad loser who stays at HQ while everyone else is enjoying themselves on tour and at the grounds. My best "memory" of touring is imagining the Barmy Army singing my carols at the Christmas Day lunch in Melbourne during the most recent Ashes tour. I really enjoyed writing that whole songbook, and it made me feel part of the tour from 12,000 miles away.'

— The Home Guard, Mike O'Sullivan, gets his Barmy Army kicks vicariously but still plays his part well.

12

NO WORDS REQUIRED – THE TUNES OF BILLY THE TRUMPET

Billy the Trumpet, aka Bill Cooper of the Royal Philharmonic Orchestra and a multitude of other august musical institutions, arrived on the Barmy Army scene by accident during the 2004 tour of the West Indies. He had no intention of becoming the Barmy Army trumpeter, but fate took a hand when he left his trumpet (that he had brought on tour purely to practise for a forthcoming concert) in a taxi. Resigned to never seeing it again, he was surprised to spot a fellow England fan playing it in the ground soon after, especially because he had lost it in Barbados and the trumpet had somehow followed him to Antigua. He went to retrieve it, was challenged to play a tune to prove it was his and the rest is history.

TOP TEN BILLY THE TRUMPET TUNES

1: 'THE GREAT ESCAPE'

This was the first song Bill ever played when challenged to prove that the trumpet was his and still the first song he plays when he pipes up now. Whether it's because *The Great Escape* used to be on TV every other Christmas when we were still limited to three channels or not, it's a tune indelibly etched on the memory of English sports fans, and for the Barmy Army it means that the fun is just about to start.

2: 'LIVIN' ON A PRAYER'

The Bon Jovi classic has become a firm Barmy Army hit, and it's not purely a Bill tune as we all sing along. The key line in the song – 'Oh! We're halfway there' – is one that can be utilised regularly during cricket matches. Got a team five wickets down? You're halfway there. Halfway to a total? Away we go. It's always enjoyable, but at its funniest when it's ironic, such as when England are chasing 500 to win and find themselves 250 for nine.

3: 'NEIGHBOURS'/'HOME AND AWAY'/
'I SHOULD BE SO LUCKY'

The poor old Aussies don't have any songs of their own and they don't have a trumpeter of their own. The classic Aussie soap opera-related theme tunes entertain Brits and Aussies alike, but it's particularly nice when Bill plays it during a home Ashes series to make those convicts who have made an effort to support their team overseas feel like they're back home. Bill had just finished entertaining the locals by playing 'Neighbours' in the Gabba during the 2006–07 series when he was evicted from the ground and subsequently banned. Maybe he should have played 'Advance Australia Fair'.

4: 'MATCH OF THE DAY'/'GRANDSTAND'

The majority of cricket fans are general sports fans as well. And there's not a British sports fan alive who (a) doesn't know the theme tunes to *Match of the Day* and *Grandstand* and (b) hasn't sung them at the top of their voice around the house on a Saturday afternoon or evening. It's slightly less embarrassing when we all do it together and a lot more tuneful when he's playing over the top.

5: 'BULLSEYE'

At this stage you might be tempted to think that all Bill does is play TV theme tunes, especially those that are sports-related, and it's certainly true that there are a few. But there is more method to the madness here than revelling in memories of the classic darts game show and Bully's special prize. It took many years before someone figured out that it would be a good song to play whenever a player got a 50, that being the number of points you get when you score a bullseye in darts. 'Hawaii Five-O' is another Bill favourite that would have been equally apt for that milestone.

6: 'SNOOKER LOOPY'

It's not originally a TV theme tune, although the Chas 'n' Dave classic is now inextricably associated with the snooker quiz show *Big Break*. Bill had played it many times before it was suggested during the 2012 tour to Sri Lanka that this would be a great tune to play whenever England (or an individual player) is on 147. This is why you'll now see us hoping for a single instead of a boundary if someone is on 146 lest the opportunity is missed. Bill previously used it as a homage to one of our favourite umpires and namesake of one of snooker's great players, Steve Davis.

7: 'BREAD OF HEAVEN' ('*CWM RHONDDA*')

Now that Cardiff has become a regular stop-off on the England Test match circus, it pays to have a tune to keep the locals happy and, with a smattering of Welsh fans in the Barmy Army ranks, this is one to show that it's not all about England. In truth, few of the English know the tune that well or are able to sing any of it, but that's exactly why we have Bill around.

8: 'ROCKY'

Bill is a big fan of the classic underdog-dun-good theme tune and used to play it to gee up the bowlers. It's had the occasional outing when players have been known to get a bit feisty in the middle, but the most memorable rendition was when Jimmy Savile was thrown out of the ground in Adelaide during the 2010–11 Ashes before regaining entry and running up the steps at the back of the stand à la Mr Stallone.

9: 'SINGING IN THE RAIN'/'SUMMER HOLIDAY'/ 'RAINDROPS KEEP FALLING ON MY HEAD'

Watch enough cricket and at some point you're going to find yourself kicking your heels while the rain falls. This was particularly true of the 2007 tour to Sri Lanka where torrential downfalls fell as often as England wickets during the last Test in Galle (England were bowled out for 81 in the first innings). During the final Test of the 2005 Ashes, when England just needed just a draw to win the series, rain breaks were welcomed by England fans as if wickets had fallen. As one fan put it: 'If I'd paid five hundred pounds for five days' cricket and didn't see a ball bowled, that would have been fine by me.'

10: 'THE LAST POST'

It's not strictly speaking a favourite tune, but worthy of inclusion in the list because of three poignant renditions. As the 2006–07 Ashes whitewash came to a merciful end, there was no more relevant song to play, apart from perhaps our rendition of 'We'll win again, don't know where, don't know when'. It was typical of the self-deprecating humour that shines through in tough times. Four years later, as we finally won the Ashes in Australia, the tables were turned as Bill played it for the Australians, and Chris Tremlett obliged by taking the last wicket halfway through. Sadly, the next occasion was during the UAE tour in 2012 to mark the passing of one of the Barmy Army's legends, George 'the Podge' Summerside.

The last word

The bar is emptying, the tour is over, there are no more songs to sing. It's getting late, the bar owners are clearing up around us, and in the corner Dave 'Wooders' Woodley pipes up with a song that he can't quite remember writing, or singing, but it seems apt to close the final page of this particular Barmy Army chapter.

And now, the end is near
And so we face the final curtain
My friends, we drank some beer
But we'll drink more, of that I'm certain
We lived life to the max
We sang our songs, not in a dour way
But more, much more than this
We did it our way

Yes there were times
When we all knew

That we would win

But then we'd lose

But through it all

We cheered our boys

Drank lots of beer

Made lots of noise

We were the best

We need a rest

We did it our way

All-time Top Ten songs

There was an overwhelming winner when we asked Barmy Army members to vote for their favourite Barmy Army song. In truth, it wasn't quite a song that won, more of a chant, but who are we to argue with democracy when hundreds of people have voted.

The 'Mitchell Johnson Song' took on a life of its own during the 2010-11 Ashes, and this is reflected in its position at the top of the list. The popularity of the Australia tour means the vote was bound to be skewed towards Australian songs, and it's another hit from the 2010-11 Ashes that comes in second: 'Take The Urn Home'.

'Everywhere We Go' polled 9.9 per cent of the vote to take third place, with honourable mentions to 'You All Live In A Convict Colony' and 'We Are The Army'.

Interestingly, the choice of the masses is completely at odds with the choices made by our songwriters when asked in their interviews for this book. Make of that what you will.

Poll results:

1	Mitchell Johnson Song	28.45%
2	Take The Urn Home	20.82%
3	Everywhere We Go	9.90%
4	You All Live In A Convict Colony	8.04%
5	We Are The Army	7.63%
6	Why, Why, Why Jesse Ryder	5.15%
7	Swanny Super Over	3.92%
7	Twelve Days of Christmas	3.92%
9	Deco's song	3.51%
9	In the jungle	3.51%

Acknowledgements

For their invaluable help putting this book together, thanks must first go to Giles Wellington and Gary Fulton for their immense knowledge of random lyrics, accurate pedantry when it comes to disputed words, and informed arguments over whether it should be 'century' or 'hundred' in the Ally Cook song, until I had to intervene and decide for them.

Thanks also to Dave Woodley for digging through his personal archives, Gary Taylor for his help with old classics, Dave Fradley for random comments, Adrian Raffill for being his usual helpful self and Deco for his feedback.

My special gratitude to Paul Burnham for asking me to write this book, so we can now use it as a bible and stop arguing about lyrics, and for all his support since then, and to my editor Ian Marshall for his help throughout the process.

Final thanks must go to everyone who has ever written or sung a Barmy Army song. You helped the Barmy Army become what it is today.

See you on tour.

**SIMON &
SCHUSTER**

EVERYWHERE WE WENT
Top tales from Cricket's Barmy Army

Ben Dirs

During the 2010-11 Ashes series, as a rampant England
were laying waste to Australia, exacting a measure of
revenge for 24 years of hurt Down Under, it became
clear the tourists had an advantage over the men in
the Baggy Green: England had a twelfth man.
England had the Barmy Army.

But who were they? And how had they arrived at this point?
In Ben Dirs' fascinating and hilarious official account, we
hear from all the key figures and many others who have
marched, sung, chanted, drunk, partied and had the
time of their lives under the Barmy Army banner.

ISBN 978-0-85720-836-1
PRICE £8.99